高等院校动画专业核心系列教材
主编 王建华 马振龙 副主编 何小青

动画专业英语

徐 欣 编著

中国建筑工业出版社

图书在版编目（CIP）数据

动画专业英语/徐欣编著. —北京：中国建筑工业出版社，2013.7
高等院校动画专业核心系列教材
ISBN 978-7-112-15515-6

Ⅰ.①动… Ⅱ.①徐… Ⅲ.①动画－英语－高等学校－教材 Ⅳ.①H31

中国版本图书馆 CIP 数据核字（2013）第 123961 号

责任编辑：唐　旭　陈　皓
责任校对：张　颖　王雪竹

高等院校动画专业核心系列教材
主编　王建华　马振龙　副主编　何小青
动画专业英语
徐欣　编著
*
中国建筑工业出版社出版、发行（北京西郊百万庄）
各地新华书店、建筑书店经销
北京嘉泰利德公司制版
北京云浩印刷有限责任公司印刷
*
开本：880×1230毫米　1/16　印张：10¾　字数：330千字
2013年8月第一版　2013年8月第一次印刷
定价：36.00元
ISBN 978-7-112-15515-6
　　（24069）
版权所有　翻印必究
如有印装质量问题，可寄本社退换
（邮政编码　100037）

《高等院校动画专业核心系列教材》编委会

主　编　王建华　马振龙
副主编　何小青
编　委（按姓氏笔画排序）
　　　　　王玉强　王执安　叶　蓬　刘宪辉　齐　骥　孙　峰
　　　　　李东禧　肖常庆　时　萌　张云辉　张跃起　张　璇
　　　　　邵　恒　周　天　顾　杰　徐　欣　高　星　唐　旭
　　　　　彭　璐　蒋元翰　靳　晶　魏长增　魏　武

总 序
INTRODUCTION

　　动画产业作为文化创意产业的重要组成部分，除经济功能之外，在很大程度上承担着塑造和确立国家文化形象的历史使命。

　　近年来，随着国家政策的大力扶持，中国动画产业也得到了迅猛发展。在前进中总结历史，我们发现：中国动画经历了20世纪20年代的闪亮登场，60年代的辉煌成就，80年代中后期的徘徊衰落。进入新世纪，中国经济实力和文化影响力的增强带动了文化产业的兴起，中国动画开始了当代二次创业——重新突围。2010年，动画片产量达到22万分钟，首次超过美国、日本，成为世界第一。

　　在动画产业这种井喷式发展背景下，人才匮乏已经成为制约动画产业进一步做大做强的关键因素。动画产业的发展，专业人才的缺乏，推动了高等院校动画教育的迅速发展。中国动画教育尽管从20世纪50年代就已经开始，但直到2000年，设立动画专业的学校少、招生少、规模小。此后，从2000年到2006年5月，6年时间全国新增303所高等院校开设动画专业，平均一个星期就有一所大学开设动画专业。到2011年上半年，国内大约2400多所高校开设了动画或与动画相关的专业，这是自1978年恢复高考以来，除艺术设计专业之外，出现的第二个"大跃进"专业。

　　面对如此庞大的动画专业学生，如何培养，已经成为所有动画教育者面对的现实，因此必须解决三个问题：师资培养、课程设置、教材建设。目前在所有专业中，动画专业教材建设的空间是最大的，也是各高校最重视的专业发展措施。一个专业发展成熟与否，实际上从其教材建设的数量与质量上就可以体现出来。高校动画专业教材的建设现状主要体现在以下三方面：一是动画类教材数量多，精品少。近10年来，动画专业类教材出版数量与日俱增，从最初上架在美术类、影视类、电脑类专柜，到目前在各大书店、图书馆拥有自身的专柜，乃至成为一大品种、门类。涵盖内容从动画概论到动画技法，可以说数量众多。与此同时，国内原创动画教材的精品很少，甚至一些优秀的动画教材仍需要依靠引进。二是操作技术类教材多，理论研究的教材少，而从文化学、传播学等学术角度系统研究动画艺术的教材可以说少之又少。三是选题视野狭窄，缺乏系统性、合理性、科学性。动画是一种综合性视听形式，它具有集技术、艺术和新媒介三种属性于一体的专业特点，要求教材建设既涉及技术、艺术，又涉及媒介，而目前的教材还很不理想。

　　基于以上现实，中国建筑工业出版社审时度势，邀请了国内较早且成熟开设动画专业的多家先进院校的学者、教授及业界专家，在总结国内外和自身教学经验的基础上，策划和编写了这套高等院校动画专业核心系列教材，以期改变目前此类教材市场之现状，更为满足动画学生之所需。

　　本系列教材在以下几方面力求有新的突破与特色：

　　选题跨学科性——扩大目前动画专业教学视野。动画本身就是一个跨学科专业，涉及艺术、技术，横跨美术学、传播学、影视学、文化学、经济学等，但传统的动画教材大多局限于动画本身，学科视野狭窄。本系列教材除了传统的动画理论、技法之外，增加研究动画文化、动画传播、动画产业等分册，力求使动画专业的学生能够适应多样的社会人才需求。

学科系统性——强调动画知识培养的系统性。目前国内动画专业教材建设，与其他学科相比，大多缺乏系统性、完整性。本系列教材力求构建动画专业的完整性、系统性，帮助学生系统地掌握动画各领域、各环节的主要内容。

层次兼顾性——兼顾本科和研究生教学层次。本系列教材既有针对本科低年级的动画概论、动画技法教材，也有针对本科高年级或研究生阶段的动画研究方法和动画文化理论。使其教学内容更加充实，同时深度上也有明显增加，力求培养本科低年级学生的动手能力和本科高年级及研究生的科研能力，适应目前不断发展的动画专业高层次教学要求。

内容前沿性——突出高层次制作、研究能力的培养。目前动画教材比较简略，多停留在技法培养和知识传授上，本系列教材力求在动画制作能力培养的基础上，突出对动画深层次理论的讨论，注重对许多前沿和专题问题的研究、展望，让学生及时抓住学科发展的脉络，引导他们对前沿问题展开自己的思考与探索。

教学实用性——实用于教与学。教材是根据教学大纲编写、供教学使用和要求学生掌握的学习工具，它不同于学术论著、技法介绍或操作手册。因此，教材的编写与出版，必须在体现学科特点与教学规律的基础上，根据不同教学对象和教学大纲的要求，结合相应的教学方式进行编写，确保实用于教与学。同时，除文字教材外，视听教材也是不可缺少的。本系列教材正是出于这些考虑，特别在一些教材后面附配套教学光盘，以方便教师备课和学生的自我学习。

适用广泛性——国内院校动画专业能够普遍使用。打破地域和学校局限，邀请国内不同地区具有代表性的动画院校专家学者或骨干教师参与编写本系列教材，力求最大限度地体现不同院校、不同教师的教学思想与方法，达到本系列动画教材学术观念的广泛性、互补性。

"百花齐放，百家争鸣"是我国文化事业发展的方针，本系列教材的推出，进一步充实和完善了当下动画教材建设的百花园，也必将推进动画学科的进一步发展。我们相信，只要学界与业界合力前进，力戒急功近利的浮躁心态，采取切实可行的措施，就能不断向中国动画产业输送合格的专业人才，保持中国动画产业的健康、可持续发展，最终实现动画"中国学派"的伟大复兴。

丛书主编：王建华

前言

当前,中国的动画产业发展速度越来越快,与国内外的动画交流也越来越多。如何培养具有良好外语能力的国际化动画人才已经成为高校动画人才教育的一个主要目标。本书综合了动画专业和英语教育两方面的知识,旨在有针对性地提高动画专业学生在学习和工作中运用英语的能力。本书内容涵盖了动画基础理论知识、艺术特性、团队分工和制作技术以及动画相关产业的发展等知识,在专业方面可以作为学生的动画入门百科,在英语教育方面则注重英语环境下听、说、读、写能力的培养,使学生能够借此学习到动画方面的专业词汇和固定表达方式,从而能够较为从容地阅读英语方面的相关专业书籍、资料,以及可以轻松地与国外同行进行专业交流。另外,本书还对著名的动画公司或工作室和动画电影节作了简单的介绍,目的是为了方便动画从业人员能更好地了解相关知识,以便参加国际动画大赛。

本书甄选了国外诸多专家的专业文章及动画专业最新的讲义、书籍、杂志等,内容丰富,专业词汇覆盖面广。本书注重对学生的词汇教学和阅读能力的提高,每课都设立了独立的词汇表,这样方便学生制订个性化的学习计划;安排的习题部分可以帮助学生巩固课程知识;拓展阅读和网络资料部分向学生们推荐了大量的课外阅读资料;课文参考译文可以帮助学生更好地理解原文。

本书适合高校的动画专业本、专科英语教学,也可作为动画方向研究生专业英语辅导资料,还可供广大动画爱好者参考学习。同时这本教材是作者潜心钻研教学的成果,希望对大家在动画专业的学习和发展上有一定的帮助。

目 录
CONTENTS

总序
前言

Unit 1　Animation Overview
第 1 单元　动画基础理论

1.1　The Fantasy World in Animation
　　　动画里的幻想世界 …………………001
1.2　Types of Animation
　　　动画的种类 …………………………004
1.3　Animation Industry
　　　动画产业 ……………………………009
1.4　Globalization and Chinese Animation
　　　全球化与中国动画 …………………014
1.5　The Future of Computer Animation
　　　电脑动画的未来 ……………………018

Unit 2　Principles and Methods of Animation Creation
第 2 单元　动画创作的原理和方法

2.1　Basic Principles of Animation 1
　　　动画片的基本原理（一）……………022
2.2　Basic Principles of Animation 2
　　　动画片的基本原理（二）……………030
2.3　The Production Process of 2D Animation
　　　二维动画的创作流程 ………………036
2.4　The Process of 3D Animation
　　　三维动画的创作流程 ………………044
2.5　The Process of Stop-Motion Animation
　　　定格动画的创作流程 ………………051

Unit 3　Responsibilities of Animation Makers
第 3 单元　动画制作者的职责

3.1　Animated Movie Director
　　　动画电影导演 ………………………065
3.2　Animation Scriptwriters
　　　动画编剧 ……………………………068
3.3　Animators
　　　动画师 ………………………………071
3.4　Art Director
　　　艺术总监 ……………………………074
3.5　Compositor and Editor
　　　合成师和剪辑师 ……………………076

Unit 4 Produce an Animation Film
第 4 单元 制作动画电影 081

4.1 Getting Started
  准备开始 ·················· 081
4.2 Animation Scriptwriting and Development
  动画剧本写作及发展 ·········· 085
4.3 Character Design
  角色设定 ·················· 095
4.4 Camera Language and the Storyboard
  镜头语言与故事板 ············ 101
4.5 Key, Extreme, Breakdown, and Inbetween
  关键帧、原画、过渡位置和中间画 ······ 113
4.6 Background Layouts and Paint
  背景构图与上色 ·············· 123
4.7 Post-Production
  后期制作 ·················· 132

Unit 5 International Animation Festival
第 5 单元 国际动画节 141

5.1 Annecy International Animation Film Festival (France)
  昂西国际动画节（法国） ·········· 141
5.2 Hiroshima International Animation Festival (Japan)
  广岛国际动画节（日本） ·········· 142
5.3 Zagreb World Festival of Animated Film (Croatia)
  萨格勒布国际动画电影节（克罗地亚） ···· 143
5.4 Ottawa International Animation Festival (Canada)
  渥太华国际动画节（加拿大） ········ 144
5.5 Holland Animation Film Festival
  荷兰动画电影节 ·············· 145

Unit 6 Famous Animation Studios
第 6 单元 著名动画工作室 147

6.1 Pixar Animation Studios
  皮克斯动画工作室 ············ 147
6.2 Blue Sky Studios
  蓝天工作室 ················ 149
6.3 Studio Ghibli
  吉卜力工作室 ·············· 151
6.4 Aardman Animation Studios
  阿德曼动画工作室 ············ 153

Appendix: Glossary
附录：动画专业术语表 155

参考文献 ···················· 163
后　记 ····················· 164

Unit1 Animation Overview
第 1 单元 动画基础理论

1.1 The Fantasy World in Animation
动画里的幻想世界

Text

The word animate comes from the Latin verb "animare", meaning "to make alive or to fill with breath". We can take our most childlike dreams or the wackiest worlds we can imagine and bring them to life. In animation we can completely restructure reality. We take drawings, clay, puppets, or forms on a computer screen, and we make them seem so real that we want to believe they're alive. Pure fantasy seems at home in animation, but for animation to work; the fantasy world must be so true to itself with its own unbroken rules that we are willing to believe it.

Even more than most film, animation is visual. While you're writing, try to keep a movie running inside your head. Visualize what you're writing. Keep those characters squashing and stretching, running in the air! Make the very basis of your idea visual. Tacking visuals onto an idea that isn't visual won't work. Many cartoon writers are also artists, and they begin their thinking by drawing or doodling. The best animation is action, not talking heads.

Time and space are important elements of animation. The laws of physics don't apply. Animation uses extremes—everything is exaggerated. A character is squashed flat, and two seconds later he's as good as new again. He can morph into someone else and do things that a real person couldn't possibly do. Although with today's special effects, there is little that can be done in animation that cannot be done in live-action film as well.

Words and phrases

animate   绘制动画，使有生气
wacky   古怪的，荒诞的
restructure   调整，重建，更改结构
reality   现实，实际，真实
clay   黏土
puppet   人偶，木偶，玩偶
fantasy   幻想，幻觉
visualize   可视化

morphing　变形，图像变形技术
tacking　固定住，定位
doodle　涂鸦，乱画
extremes　极端，最大程度
exaggerated　夸张的，夸大的，言过其实的
Latin verb　拉丁语动词
unbroken rule　完整的规则
squashing and stretching　挤压和拉伸（动画的 12 个基本创作原则之一，详见第 2 单元）
time and space　时间和空间（动画的 12 个基本创作原则之一，详见第 2 单元）
the laws of physics　物理定律
special effects　（电影、电视剧中的）特技效果
live-action film　真人电影

Practice

1. What's the different between animation and live-action film?
2. What does your fantasy world look like? It is wacky? Crazy? Sweet?
3. What are the important elements of animation?

Translate into English

1. 物理定律在动画里是不适用的。
2. 做动画就是将你头脑里的想法视觉化，无法转化成视觉的想法都是无法做成动画的。
3. 在动画里我们可以重新构建一个真实的世界。

Further reading

Animation from Pencils to Pixels: Classical Techniques for the Digital Animator
Editor: Tony White
Publisher: Focal Press (2006)

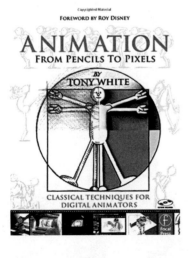

Who's Who in Animated Cartoons: An International Guide to Film and Television's Award-winning and Legendary Animators

Editor: Jeff Lenburg

Publisher: Applause Theatre Book Publishers (2006)

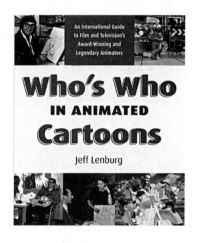

The World History of Animation

Editor: Stephen Cavalier

Publisher: University of California Press (2011)

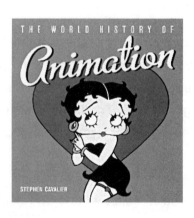

Web links

www.historyanimated.com

Translation of text

　　动画一词来源于拉丁语，意思是"使其鲜活或用呼吸来填补"。我们可以把最有童趣的梦境或能想象出来的最古怪的世界变成现实。在动画里我们可以完全重建一个真实的世界。我们可以用图画、黏土、人偶或在电脑屏幕上的各种形式,使它们看起来如此真实以至于我们愿意相信它们是活生生的。在动画里,纯粹幻想可以任意想象，但是将动画作为工作,幻想世界自身就必须有真实性,有完整的规则,这样我们就愿意相信它是真的。

　　动画完全是视觉享受，从这点来说甚至超过大多数的电影。当你在为动画写剧本的时候，要尽量将运动的影像保持在头脑里，把你的写作视觉化。想象着角色如何拉长、压扁，如何在空中奔跑！将你最基本的想法可视化。不能被视觉化的想法是没有用的。很多动画编剧同时也是画家，他们经常通过绘画或涂鸦来开始他们的创意。好的动画是对动作的表现，而不是只画一个会说话的脑袋。

　　时间和空间是动画片的重要元素。物理定律在动画里是不适用的。动画用极端的表达方式来表现，所有的东西都是夸张的。一个角色被压扁了，两秒钟后他又会恢复原状。他可以变形成为其他人，并且可以做真人做不到的事情。尽管如今的特效制作已经很厉害了，但是真人电影无法实现的东西动画却可以做得到。

1.2　Types of Animation
动画的种类

Text

　　There are many different types of animation in the world. Generally animation can be broken down into three main categories: traditional animation, stop motion animation, computer animation. All of these have their own distinct attributes.

Traditional Animation

　　Traditional animation (or classical animation, cel animation, or hand-drawn animation), is an animation technique where each frame is drawn by hand. In the traditional animation process, animators will begin by drawing sequences of animation on sheets of transparent paper perforated to fit the peg bars in their desks, often using colored pencils, one picture or "frame" at a time. A peg bar is an animation tool that is used in traditional animation to keep the drawings in place. Traditional animation is a very expensive and time-consuming process; the technique was the dominant form of animation in cinema until the advent of computer animation.

　　The current process, termed "digital ink and paint", is the same as traditional ink and paint until after the animation drawings are completed; instead of being transferred to cels by hand, the outline drawings are scanned into a computer, where they are colored and processed using one or more of a variety of software packages. The resulting drawings composited in a computer program on many transparent "layers" much the same way as they are with cels, and made into a sequence of images which may then be transferred onto film or converted to a digital video format. It is now also possible for animators to draw directly into a computer using a graphics tablet, where the outline drawings are done in a similar manner as they would be on paper.

　　Computers and digital video cameras can also be used as tools in traditional animation without affecting the film directly, assisting the animators in their work and making the whole process faster and easier. For example, doing the layouts on a computer is much more effective than doing it by traditional methods. Though traditional animation is now commonly done with computers, it is important to differentiate computer-assisted traditional animation from 3D computer animation, such as Toy Story and Ice Age. However, often traditional animation and 3D computer animation will be used together, as Disney's Tarzan and Treasure Planet. Most anime still use traditional animation today.

Stop Motion Animation

Stop motion (also known as stop frame) is an animation technique to make objects appear to move on their own. The object is moved in small increments between individually photographed frames, creating the illusion of movement when the series of frames is played as a continuous sequence. A model with movable joints, clay figures or puppet are often used in stop motion for their ease of repositioning, moving an object slightly and for each slight movement shooting a frame at a time, with tiny changes in position being made between each frame. Not all stop motion requires figures or models; many stop motion films can involve using humans, household appliances and other things for comedic effect.

There are many different types of stop motion animation, usually named after the type of material used to create the animation, such as clay animation, cutout animation, graphic animation, model animation, object animation, puppet animation, etc..

Computer Animation

Modern computer animation or CGI animation is the latest technique of animation that includes 2D and 3D animation. In the process, computers can be used to entirely create the shapes and colors for generating animated images by using software, working from a series of mathematical codes, or they can be used to enhance traditional animation.

Computer animation is essentially a digital successor to the stop motion techniques used in traditional animation with 3D models and frame-by-frame animation of 2D illustrations. Computer generated animations are more controllable than other more physically based processes, such as constructing miniatures for effects shots or hiring extras for crowd scenes, and because it allows the creation of images that would not be feasible using any other technology. It can also allow a single graphic artist to produce such content without the use of actors, expensive set pieces, or props.

For 3D animation, objects (models) are built on the computer monitor and 3D figures are rigged with a virtual skeleton, all frames must be rendered after modeling is complete. For 2D figure animations, separate objects (illustrations) and separate transparent layers are used, with or without a virtual skeleton. Then the limbs, eyes, mouth, clothes, etc. of the figure are moved by the animator on key frames. The differences in appearance between key frames are automatically calculated by the computer in a process known as tweening or morphing. Finally, the animation is rendered.

Words and phrases

category   类别，分类

frame　帧，电影画面
sequence　序列，一连串
sheet　纸张，（一）片，一张纸
perforated　打孔的，有排孔的
outline　轮廓，大纲，概述，描画……轮廓
format　格式，版本
layout　布局，构图，安排
computer-assisted　计算机辅助的
anime　日本动画
illusion　幻觉，错觉
joint　关节，接缝，接合处
miniature　缩图，微型画，微型图画绘画术
prop　道具
rig　装配，绑定
virtual　虚拟的
skeleton　骨骼，骨架
render　渲染，着色
calculate　计算
tweening　补间动画，中间计算
morphing　变形，图像变形技术
traditional animation　传统动画，有着一系列的制作工序，它首先要将动画镜头中每一个动作的关键部分先设计出来，也就是要先画出原画，根据原画再画出中间画，即动画，然后还需要经过一张张地描线、上色、逐张逐帧地拍摄录制等过程。
stop motion animation　定格动画，停格动画
computer animation　电脑动画，计算机动画，利用电脑生成的图像制作出来的动画
classical animation　经典动画
cel animation　赛璐珞动画
hand-drawn animation　手绘动画
peg bar　动画定位尺
graphics tablet　数码绘图板，图形输入板
Toy Story　《玩具总动员》，1995年由华特·迪士尼影片公司和皮克斯动画工作室合作推出，是第一部完全电脑动画制作的电影长片。
Ice Age　《冰河世纪》，一部由20世纪福克斯公司和蓝天工作室在2002年合作推出的三维动画。
Tarzan　《人猿泰山》，1999年上映的迪士尼第37部经典长篇剧情动画，采用了二维与三维结合的制作方法。
Treasure Planet　《星银岛》，2002年迪士尼公司推出的第42部经典动画电影，采用了二维与三维结合的制作方法。
comedic effect　喜剧效果

clay animation 黏土动画
cutout animation 剪纸动画
graphic animation 图形动画
model animation 模型动画
object animation 实体动画
puppet animation 偶动画
mathematical codes 数学编程
frame-by-frame 逐帧
set piece 场景，舞台立体布景
key frame 关键帧

Practice

1. What are the three main categories of modern animation?
2. What is computer's influence on the traditional animation?
3. What's the principle of stop motion animation?

Translate into English

1. 在传统动画制作过程当中，动画定位尺是用来固定定位纸的。
2. 如今电脑也会应用在传统动画中，其作用是辅助制作。
3. 在三维软件里，要先创建人物模型，然后将虚拟的骨架与模型进行绑定。

Further reading

Moving Innovation: A History of Computer Animation
Editor: Tom Sito
Publisher: MIT Press (2013)

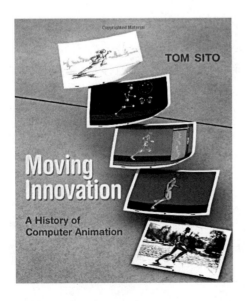

Web links

www.the-flying-animator.com

Translation of text

动画的类型有多种多样，大体来说动画可以分为三大类：传统动画、定格动画和电脑动画。所有这些类别的动画都拥有自己独特的特性。

传统动画

传统动画（或称做古典动画、赛璐珞动画、手绘动画），这个动画技术是由手绘来完成每一帧的制作。在传统动画的制作过程当中，动画师将一系列的动画内容绘制在透明的赛璐珞片上，并固定在桌子上的动画定位尺上，通常使用彩色铅笔来绘制，一次完成一张图片或"一格"。动画定位尺是一种动画工具，专门用在传统动画里以固定动画定位纸。传统动画是一个非常耗费财力和时间的过程，这种形式在电脑动画问世之前一直都是影院动画片的主力。

在动画制作过程中，被称为"数字上色和绘制"的这个步骤和传统的上色绘制是一样的，这种方法替代了用手将动画转描到赛璐珞片上，动画的线描稿被扫描进电脑里，然后用一个或多种软件来上色及完成其他步骤。由此产生的图形接着在电脑里与很多透明的"层"进行合成，这个过程与赛璐珞片很相似，接着就可以制作出一组序列帧图片，这些图片可以输出成胶片或者数字格式的视频文件。现在技术的发展可以使动画师用手绘板直接在电脑上绘制线稿，就像在纸上绘制线稿一样。

电脑和数码录像机也可以作为传统动画的辅助工具，它们不直接影响动画制作，只是帮助动画师完成工作，使整个制作过程更快、更容易。例如，在电脑上制作构图设计比传统方法有效得多。虽然现在传统动画一般都用电脑来完成，但是区别电脑辅助传统动画和三维电脑动画是很重要的，像《玩具总动员》、《冰河世纪》就是标准的三维电脑动画。然而，往往传统动画和三维电脑动画会结合在一起使用，例如迪士尼的《泰山》和《星银岛》。大部分的日本动画仍然使用传动动画的方法。

定格动画

定格（又称做"停格"）是一种操控对象或者对象自己产生动作的动画技术。物体在拍摄下来的帧与帧之间做小幅度的移动，这样系列帧连续播放的时候就会产生运动的视觉效果。有活动关节的模型、黏土角色或者人偶，因为它们很方便做动作定位，所以经常用在定格动画里，轻轻地移动角色对象，每做一个细微的动作就拍摄一帧，每帧之间在位置上都要有细小的变化。不是所有的定格动画都需要角色或者模型，很多定格电影也包括使用真人、家用电器和其他东西来做出喜剧效果。

定格动画也有很多不同的种类，通常根据所使用的材料类型来命名，像黏土动画、剪纸动画、图形动画、模型动画、实体动画、偶动画等。

电脑动画

现代电脑动画或CGI动画是动画领域最新的技术，其中包括二维和三维两大部分。在电脑制作过程中，通过使用电脑软件可以给生成的动画图像创造图形和颜色，这些是由一系列的数字编程完成的，这些程序运算也可以用来辅助传统动画的制作。

电脑动画本质上是传统动画里所使用的定格技术的数字化继承者，使用三维模型以及逐帧动画的二维图形来制作三维动画。电脑生成动画比其他基于物理现象的动画制作过程都容易控制，比如给特效镜头创建缩微模型或者大规模的场景，因为电脑可以允许创建任何的图像，而这些在其他技术里是无法实现的。电脑也可以让一个艺术家在没有演员、昂贵场景、道具的情况下独立完成一部作品。

做三维动画，对象（模型）的创建是在电脑显示器上进行操作演示的，三维的角色用虚拟的骨架来进行绑定，所有帧都必须在建模完成之后才能进行渲染。针对二维角色动画，要用独立的对象（图像）和独立的透明图层，虚拟的骨架有时候需要用，也有时候不用。然后角色的四肢、眼睛、嘴、衣服等这些部分由动画师来移动并设置关键帧。帧与帧之间的差别将由电脑自动运算，这个过程被称为补间动画或变形。最后，动画就可以被渲染出来。

1.3 Animation Industry
动画产业

Text

Cultural economics is recognized as a new field of economics. It offers a new perspective for looking at the characteristics of cultural goods and services, implementation of cultural policies, finance of the art and diverse forms of cultural industries. Animation is one of the most influential, active and rapidly developing cultural industries in the world. It is one of the fastest-growing fields in film and television, and it is also integral to video games and web development. The content and styles of animations have been expanded towards more diverse audiences including children, teenagers, adults and family. The demand for animated entertainment has expanded with the increase in broadcasting hours by cable and satellite TV along with the growing popularity of the Internet. At present, North America, Japan and Korea are the world's top three animation producers and profit gainers. This chapter will provide an overview of the animation industries in these three countries which includes their well-known animation products, typical characters' images, development directions and government policies.

Animation Industry in North America

In North America, there are eight major animation producers, Disney, DreamWorks SKG, Warner Brother, Sony Picture Entertainment, Fox Entertainment Group, Paramount Pictures, Lucas Film and Universal Studio. They are very dominant in the market and make the U.S. the world's largest animation kingdom. Within this sector, the annual income exceeds 1,000 hundred million dollars. In addition to its artistic and technological success, America is also the first country to bring animation into the commercial market and form a large scale world industry. The American animation industry has a very careful labor division and complete production chain. However, this sector is not under the control of an individual institution. Instead, it is united by the eight top animation companies which were mentioned before. These eight companies have their own newspapers, magazines, TV stations and satellite cables, which enable them to produce their work as independent transmitter. Disney, for instance, is the most successful animation producers in North America and the world. It produces animations, forms famous animated cartoon characters and even builds its own animation kingdom – Disney land. It has the achieved dream of transferring joys into the monetary terms and it has gained a great deal of success in the world.

Animation Industry in Japan

Currently, Japan is the second largest animation industry in the world and has gained great success since the 1990's. The content of Japanese animation is more complex than the American one. It emphasizes reflection on the character's inner senses, psychological struggles and complex social realities. The most peculiar characteristic of the Japanese animation market is its diversity and detailed subdivision among audiences. In Japan, there are animations and Manga that are able to satisfy all types of audiences with diverse occupations and lifestyles. They are automatically divided up by producers themselves.

The Japanese animation industry, just like that of North America, has a perfect industrial chain. However, its starting point is different from that of North America. Most Japanese animations are derived from the top selling comic books, known as "Manga" in Japanese, which lowers the risk of having a low viewing rate after broadcasting and at the same time stimulates the development of Manga and other animation-related merchandise. In Japan, a company does not have to have the finance to produce an animation; all they have to do is to look for sponsors, including TV stations, magazines, publications etc.. In this way of investing in animation, the project will be evaluated or suggested by specialists in this field in its preliminary stages, which lowers the investors' risks. Moreover, government support has also helped the development of Japanese animation. The Japanese government imposed low taxation on exporting domestic animations; established the Tokyo Animation Centre in 2003 and many other similar institutions in order to promote the development of domestic animation and it has financed them when necessary. In the mean time, Japanese animation fans organize different activities such as Costume Play (Cosplay) to create a platform to stimulate their own favorite animation characters. Every year, Cosplay shops make a lot of valuable profits from this type of animation-related activity. Until now, Cosplay has had a great impact in many other Asian countries.

Animation Industry in Korea

Korea is the most famous Asian animation manufacture after Japan. In 2003, the output of the Korean animation industry reached around 2.7 hundred million dollars, which occupied 0.4% of the world market. Although this number is not comparable with Japanese animations, the Korean animation industry is still growing and forming its own style and operation system. Instead of putting animations on TV and cinema, Korean animators and producers take advantage of the global communication platform-internet, and extensively produce Korean made Flashes by using 2D and 3D computer technologies.

The success of the Korean animation industry is attributed to the fully support of the government.

In the 1980's the Korean government had already started to assist domestic animation in order to expand its cultural industry. In 2003, the Korean government provided 2 hundred million dollars to help increase the output of domestic animations and established a non-government organization to analyze the domestic market and give advice to investors and producers. Moreover, along with other Asian countries, Korea also confronts the challenges of imported animations from Japan and America. In order to create a fine industrial environment for the domestic animation, the Korean government once again implemented a policy on limiting the broadcasting rates between Korean, Japanese and other animations as 45%, 33%, 22%. In addition, the Korean government stipulated that each TV station needed to use 1%~1.5% of total time to broadcast domestic animation in order to protect Korean animations. The government also controls the content and divisions among animation products, which is called Korea Media Rating Board.

Words and phrases

perspective   透视，观点，角度
implementation   实现，履行，安装启用
sector   行业，部门
commercial   商业的，营利的
institution   制度，建立
monetary   货币的，金钱的
Manga   日本漫画
stimulate   刺激，鼓舞，激励
merchandise   商品，货物
sponsor   赞助商，赞助单位
publication   出版，出版物
taxation   征税，税款
domestic   国内的，国产的，本土的
platform   平台
stipulate   规定
cable and satellite TV   有线电视，卫星电视

Disney   全称为 The Walt Disney Company，取名自其创始人华特·迪士尼，是总部设在美国伯班克的大型跨国公司，主要业务包括娱乐节目制作、主题公园、玩具、图书、电子游戏和传媒网络。

DreamWorks SKG   梦工厂，是美国排名前十位的一家电影洗印、制作和发行公司，同时也是一家电视游戏、电视节目制作公司。

Warner Brother   华纳兄弟娱乐公司，全称 Warner Bros. Entertainment Inc.，是全球最大的电影和电视娱乐制作公司。

Sony Picture Entertainment   索尼影视娱乐有限公司，是索尼（美国）有限公司（SCA）的子公司，在全球的业务包括：电影的制作和发行，电视节目的制作和发行，数码娱乐节目的制作和发行，全球范围的电视频道投资，购买和发行家庭娱乐节目，经营影视拍摄设施，开发新型娱乐产品、服务和技术，

以及在 67 个国家进行电影娱乐产品销售。

Fox Entertainment Group　福克斯娱乐集团，是美国娱乐产业公司，旗下包括电影制片厂、无线电视、有线电视以及卫星广播电视产业。

Paramount Pictures　派拉蒙影业公司，美国电影制片和发行公司。

Lucas Film　卢卡斯影业，卢卡斯影业有限公司是乔治·卢卡斯于 1971 年在加利福尼亚州旧金山建立的美国电影公司。该公司是电影行业视觉特效、声音特效和计算机动画的业界领袖，由于他们出色的专业技术，他们的子公司经常协助其他的电影制作公司工作。

Universal Studio　环球影城

production chain　生产链，流水线

Disney land　迪士尼乐园

psychological struggle　心理斗争

social reality　社会现实

Tokyo Animation Centre　东京动画中心

non-government organization　民间组织，非政府组织

Practice

1. How do you think Cosplay?
2. What did Korean government do for supporting and protecting domestic animation?
3. What are the eight major animation producers in North America?

Translate into English

1. 动画是在世界上最有影响力、发展速度最快的文化产业之一。
2. 日本动画的内容比美国动画更复杂，它强调反映人物内心的感觉、心理斗争和复杂的社会现实。
3. 政府的支持有力地帮助了日本动画的发展。

Further reading

Animation—Art and Industry: A Reader

Editor: Maureen Furniss

Publisher: John Libbey Cinema and Animation (2009)

Web links

www.animeherald.com

Translation of text

  文化经济是经济学的一个新领域。它为看待文化产品和服务、实施文化政策以及不同形式的文化产业提供了一个全新的视角。动画是在世界上最有影响力、最活跃、发展速度最快的文化产业之一。它也是在电影和电视行业中增长最快的领域之一，同时在视频游戏和网页开发领域中也是不可或缺的。动画的内容和风格已经扩大面向更多元化的观众，包括儿童、青少年、成人和家庭。随着有线电视和卫星电视广播时间的增加，以及互联网的日益普及，动画的娱乐需求在不断地扩大。目前，美国、日本及韩国是世界顶级的三大动画生产和利润所得国。这一小节将介绍动画产业在这三个国家的概况，包括知名的动漫产品、典型的角色形象、发展方向及政府的政策。

美国动画产业

  在美国，有八个主要的动画生产商，迪士尼、梦工厂SKG、华纳兄弟、索尼影视娱乐、福克斯娱乐集团、派拉蒙影业公司、卢卡斯电影和环球影城。他们在市场上占有主导地位，使美国成为世界上最大的动画王国。在这个行业，年收入超过1000亿美元。除了其艺术和技术上的成功，美国也是第一个将动画带入商业市场并形成了一个巨大规模产业的国家。美国动画产业有着非常细致的分工和完整的生产链。然而，这个行业并不是在一个单独的机构的控制之下。相反的，是由之前提到的八个顶级动画公司联合掌控的。这八家公司有自己的报纸、杂志、电视台和卫星电缆，他们可以生产自己的动画节目并独立传播。例如，迪士尼是在北美乃至世界上最成功的动画生产商。它制作动画，塑造著名的动画卡通人物，甚至建立了自己的动画王国——迪士尼乐园。它实现了将快乐转化成货币形式的梦想，并且取得了巨大的成功。

日本动画产业

  目前，日本是世界上第二大动画产业国，1990年代以来已经获得了巨大的成功。日本动画的内容比美国更复杂。它强调反映人物的内心感觉、心理斗争和复杂的社会现实。日本动漫市场最特别的就是其多样性及对观众类别极其详细的划分。在日本，动画和漫画能够满足各类不同职业和生活方式的观众的需要。它们会由动画生产商自己来划分。

  日本动画产业就像美国一样，拥有完美的产业链。但是它的出发点与美国不同。大多数日本动画都来源于最畅销的漫画书，在日本被称为"Manga"，从而降低了播出后会有低收视率的风险，并且同时刺激漫画和动画相关商品的发展。在日本，一个动画公司不会自己出资金来制作动画，他们所要做的是寻找赞助商，包括电视台、杂志、出版物等。

  以这种投资动画的方式，一个项目会在它的起步阶段由该领域的专家来进行评估或提出建议，从而降低投资者的风险。此外，政府的支持也有力地帮助了日本动画的发展。日本政府对出口国内动画实施低税率，在2003年设立了东京动画中心和许多其他类似机构，以促进国产动画的发展，并在必要时资助它们。与此同时，日本的动漫迷们举办不同的活动，如角色扮演（Cosplay），以此来搭建一个平台模仿自己喜爱的动画人物。因为从这种动画相关活动中，角色扮演店每年都会有一笔很大的收入。直到现在，角色扮演已经对许多亚洲其他国家产生了很大的影响。

韩国动画产业

韩国是继日本之后亚洲最有名的动画生产国家。在 2003 年，韩国动漫产业的产量达到约 2.7 亿美元，占世界市场的 0.4%。虽然这个数字不能与日本动画相比较，但是韩国的动漫产业仍在增长并形成了自己的风格和运作体系。韩国的动画师和生产商利用全球通信平台网络来发布动画，从而取代了将动画投放在电视上和电影院里，并利用二维和三维计算机技术大量制作韩国风格的 Flash 动画短片。

韩国动画产业的成功归因于政府的大力支持。韩国政府在 1980 年就已经开始资助本土动画以此扩大其文化产业。在 2003 年，韩国政府提供了 2 亿美元来帮助提高本土动画产量，并成立了一个非政府组织来分析国内市场，并给投资者和生产商以建议。此外，与其他亚洲国家一样，韩国也面临着来自日本和美国的进口动画的挑战。为了给本土动画创造良好的产业环境，韩国政府再次实施一项政策，限制韩国、日本及其他国家动画之间的播放比例为 45%、33% 和 22%。另外，韩国政府规定各电视台需要用总时间的 1%~1.5% 来播出本土动画，以此来保护韩国动画。韩国政府还控制动漫产品的内容和分类，负责这项工作的部门是韩国媒体评级委员会。

1.4 Globalization and Chinese Animation
全球化与中国动画

Text

Animation Industry in China

Animation is targeted as one of the most important industries for pushing Chinese cultural economics forward. According to China's Animation Industry Report (2004-2005), animations have a large market sector, and its derivatives are tremendously beneficial. In recent times, the animation industry has grown rapidly in mainland China. However, the flourishing surface hides awkwardness in the background. Although the gross income of the Chinese animation industry already exceeded that of the film industry, because of its tremendous market and lack of creativity, more than 80 percent of the profits that generated from animation industry were trapped into the pockets of Japanese and Americans. As a result, China became the world's largest import country for animation products.

According to the Report of Chinese Cultural Industry Development (2012), currently, under the impact of globalization, the development of Chinese domestic animations has fallen into two strange loops. These are economic and cultural loops. First of all, along with the expansion of globalization, because animation is a unique form of artistic expression, it crosses national and cultural borders, and spreads out across the world. After Japan and America won a great deal of success and reclaimed the initial costs for making animations domestically, they sat out to explore the international market and by ways of low or free price strategy entered into the Chinese market, which has left the Chinese domestic animation industry falling into an economic loop.

Secondly, the imported animations, at the same time as creating an economic loop in the Chinese animation market, also bring about a cultural loop. In the last 20 years, these imported animation works have changed the desires and tendencies of Chinese audiences. Following the popularity of televisions in the late 1980's, more and more foreign-styled entertainments have emerged into China. When imported animation characters and plot styles are deeply engraved on Chinese audiences' memories, they unconsciously change the aesthetic standards among audiences. In turn they become the referential standards for audiences to judge the quality of animations and guide them to consume in the future. In China, many adults still narrow mindedly consider animation as an entertainment for children. However, they neglect the impact of imported animations on the younger generations. By consuming imported animations, children and young people will unconsciously accept the value and life styles that foreign animations present to them. In the long term, the values of foreign cultures and life styles from imported animations may play a dominant role and further replace the original cultural values among Chinese youth.

Government Support

Government plays a decisive role in helping a new industry to develop, especially in its preliminary stage. Although in the 1990's, the Chinese government paid close attention to the development of domestic animation, in 2000, this field was officially defined as an industry by the government and in 2001 the state decided to develop it in the long term as a part of the domestic economy. In 2004, the State Administration of Radio Film and Television (SARFT) produced an official document, which indicated that each permitted animation channel must broadcast at least 50% of animated programs within 24 hours/day and that among them domestic animations should not be less than 60% of the broadcasted material. In addition, every imported animation must be checked first by the regional government and then reviewed again by the SARFT before it is broadcasted. Moreover, any international animation related activities must be permitted by the SARFT, otherwise, they are considered as illegal. On 29th April 2006, the state council officially determined the animation industry as a high technology industry, and started to reduce its taxation. In 2006, SARFT officially forbade any TV station to broadcast imported animations between 17:00 and 20:00. Therefore, when no imported animations are broadcast during this "Golden Time", the only option is to watch the domestic ones. Moreover, in order to address different principles and regulations to protect the domestic animation industry, the Chinese government also allocates funds to encourage establishing animation academies; exploring more diverse animation bases since 2001.

According to the policies and principles issued by the Chinese government in recent years regarding the domestic animation market, it is clear that animation will be developed as an industry to serve the wider audiences instead of being treated as only children's entertainment. In order to regain the lost domestic animation market in both economic and cultural respects, the Chinese government requires an increased volume of domestic animations as a strategy to develop the domestic animation industry.

Words and phrases

derivatives 衍生产品
beneficial 有益的，有利的
awkwardness 尴尬
exceeded 超过，胜过
import 输入，进口
globalization 全球化
loop 循环，圈，环
reclaim 要求收回
strategy 战略，策略
tendency 趋势，癖好，意向
unconsciously 不知不觉，无意识地
neglect 疏忽，忽视
council 理事会，委员会
regain 收复，取回
China's Animation Industry Report 中国动画产业报告
mainland China 中国内地
flourishing surface 繁荣的表面
lack of creativity 缺乏创意的
trap into 诱骗……使之采取某种行动
Chinese Cultural Industry Development 中国文化产业发展
aesthetic standard 审美标准
narrow mindedly 目光短浅
State Administration of Radio Film and Television 广播电影电视总局
regional government 地方政府

Practice

1. What's your idea about the major defects in Chinese animation industry?
2. What is the impact of globalization on Chinese animation?

Translate into English

1. 过去的十几年，外国动画在一定程度上改变了中国观众的审美标准。
2. 中国动画产业在繁荣的表象下面隐藏着很多的问题。

Further reading

Annual Report on Development of China's Animation Industry (2011)
中国动漫产业发展报告 (2011)

Editor: 卢斌，郑玉明，牛兴侦
Publisher: 社会科学文献出版社

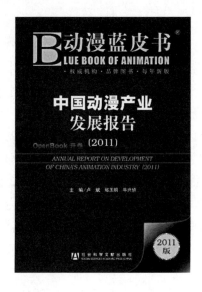

Web links

www.researchinchina.com

Translation of text

中国动画产业

动画是推动中国文化经济发展最重要的产业之一。据《中国动漫产业发展报告》(2004—2005年)所述，动画有着很大的市场需求，而且动漫衍生品的利润空间也是非常大的。在最近几年，中国内地的动漫产业发展迅速。然而，在繁荣的表象之下也隐藏着很多问题。虽然中国动漫产业的总收入已经超过了电影业，但是由于其巨大的市场和本土动画缺乏创意，动漫产业产生的利润的80%以上进入日本人和美国人的口袋。其结果就是中国成为世界上最大的动漫产品进口国。

据《中国文化产业发展报告》(2012年)所述，目前在全球化的影响下，中国国产动画的发展已陷入两个奇怪的循环，即经济和文化的循环。首先，由于动画是一种独特的艺术表现形式，随着全球化的扩张它跨越国家和文化的边界，扩散到世界各地。日本和美国的动画产业获得了巨大的成功，并在收回动画制作成本之后，他们开始开拓国际市场，以低价或免费策略进入中国市场，这样就使中国国产动画行业落入一个经济循环。

其次，进口动画在中国动画市场制造了经济循环的同时也带来了文化循环。在过去的20年中，这些进口动画作品改变了中国观众的要求和喜好。随着1980年代后期电视的普及，越来越多的外国风格的娱乐节目进入中国。进口动画的角色和情节风格深深地刻在中国观众的记忆里，它们在不知不觉之中改变了观众的审美标准。反过来，它们成为观众判断动画质量的参照标准，并将在未来引导他们的消费方式。在中国，许多成年人仍然单纯地认为动画只是儿童的娱乐方式。然而，他们忽略了进口动画对年轻一代

的影响。通过消费进口动画，儿童和年轻人会不自觉地接受外国动画呈现给他们的价值观和生活方式。从长远来看，进口动画在传播外国文化价值观和生活方式中发挥了主导作用，并会进一步取代中国青年原来的文化价值观。

政府的支持

政府的支持和帮助对一个新产业的发展起着决定性的作用，尤其是在起步阶段。在1990年代，中国政府曾密切关注国产动画的发展，在2000年这一领域由政府正式定义为一个行业，并于2001年决定将它作为国内经济的一部分进行长期的开发。2004年，国家广播电影电视总局（广电总局）发布正式文件，每个允许的动画频道24小时/天的电视节目里至少要有50%的动画节目，其中国产动画不应少于60%。此外，每部进口动画片必须先由地区政府进行审查，然后在正式播出之前由广电总局再次审查。此外，任何国际动漫的相关活动也必须由广电总局审查通过，否则将被视为非法活动。2006年4月29日，国务院正式确定动漫产业为高科技产业，并开始减少其税收。在2006年，广电总局正式禁止任何电视台在17:00至20:00之间播出进口动画。因此，在"黄金时段"没有进口动画播出的情况下，唯一的选择就是收看国产动画片。此外，为了实施不同的政策和法规来保护国内的动漫产业，从2001年开始中国政府还拨款鼓励建立动画学院，开发动漫基地。

从近年来中国政府颁布的国内动漫市场政策和法规来看，动画显然被作为一个服务于更广泛的受众的行业来开发，而不是仅被视为儿童的娱乐。为了在经济和文化方面夺回失去的国内动漫市场，中国政府要求将增加国产动画的产量作为发展国内动漫产业的一项重要策略。

1.5 The Future of Computer Animation
电脑动画的未来

Text

When it comes to entertainment in the modern era, animation is big business. Since the release of Toy Story in 1995, Walt Disney Pictures and Pixar Animation Studios have released 12 computer animated features which have collectively grossed a staggering $4 billion. The success of the Dreamworks-produced Shrek franchise and other computer animated films like Ice Age and Happy Feet have only served further notice that computer animation will be the dominant form of animation in the future, edging out traditional 2D animation. Until recently, computer animation dealt primarily with 2D graphics. Increasingly, however, and as the technology advances and software programs grow in capability, 3D graphics are playing a larger part in the creation of computer animation.

One of the main challenges facing animators in the immediate future is how to depict humans in computer animation: after all, most animated films deal with animal characters (Finding Nemo) or anthropomorphized objects (Cars) (Fact: the average animated film takes about four years to complete from start to finish).

The main challenge facing contemporary animators lies in their ability to depict human beings realistically, with all the natural movements, biomechanics, and sheer physics of natural life authentically reproduced. Because of the widely understood difficulty of doing so, animating a "photorealistic human being" is considered the "holy grail" of the animation industry today. This was not the case with traditional hand-drawn animation, in which artists were free to experiment with character designs.

And then there is the fact that computer animation extends far beyond the domain of family features: films like King Kong, Spider-man, Pirates of the Caribbean, and the Lord of the Rings trilogies relied heavily on computer animation in virtually every aspect of their production, from character design to physical simulation. Video games, of course, also incorporate various aspects of computer animation and graphics design.

A common criticism from animation purists of computer animation is that it is simply an exercise in technological know-how, and that it has all but obliterated story-based hand-drawn animated features. Despite the recent plethora of computer animated films, the fact is that traditional animation is far from over. The Simpsons Movie, which was released in 2007, was a huge hit, making it the biggest animated grosser since Disney's Lilo & Stitch in 2002. And the success of Disney's Enchanted (which featured a 10-minute hand-drawn animated introduction) proves that the medium has retained a lot of its power. Disney was also well into production on its first fully traditionally animated 2D feature since 2004. Called the Princess and the Frog, the film features Disney's first black princess and was released in December 2009.

Words and phrases

    release　发布
    depict　描述，描画
    anthropomorphize　赋予人性，人格化
    contemporary　当代的
    biomechanics　生物力学，生物机械学
    photorealistic　相片般逼真的
    criticism　批评，批判
    obliterate　去除，删除，彻底破坏
    story-based　故事为本
    plethora　过多，过剩
    modern era　现代
    edge out　挤掉，险胜
    authentically reproduce　真实地再现
    holy grail　必杀技

Pixar Animation Studios　皮克斯动画工作室，总部坐落于美国加利福尼亚州的埃默里维尔，一直致力于制作优秀的电脑动画作品，公司的作品多次获得奥斯卡最佳动画短片奖、最佳动画长片奖以及其他技术类奖项。

Shrek　《怪物史莱克》，梦工厂于2003年出品的三维动画长片。

Happy Feet　《快乐的大脚》，华纳兄弟于2006年出品的三维动画长片。

Finding Nemo 《海底总动员》，迪士尼和皮克斯于 2003 年出品的三维动画长片。
Cars 《汽车总动员》，迪士尼和皮克斯于 2006 年出品的三维动画长片。
King Kong 《金刚》，2005 年上映的冒险电影。
Spider-man 《蜘蛛侠》，哥伦比亚影业公司于 2002 年出品的动作片。
Pirates of the Caribbean 《加勒比海盗》，迪士尼于 2003 年出品的冒险电影。
the Lord of the Rings trilogies 《指环王》三部曲，由导演彼得·杰克逊执导的系列电影。
Enchanted 《魔法奇缘》，迪士尼于 2007 年出品的剧情片，真人拍摄与二维动画相结合。
Princess and the Frog 《公主与青蛙》，由迪士尼于 2009 年制作的第 49 部经典动画长片电影。

Practice

1. Which do you like, 2D animation or 3D computer animation? And why?
2. What is the most important thing for animation, story or technology?

Translate into English

1. 在动画里最具挑战的事情就是制作出逼真的人物。
2. 动画的功能已经远远超出了家庭娱乐的范围。

Further reading

The Art of 3D Computer Animation and Effects
Editor: Isaac Victor Kerlow
Publisher: John Wiley & Sons Inc.; 4th Revised Edition (2009)

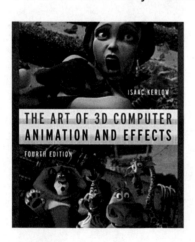

Web links

www.siggraph.org

Translation of text

每当谈及当今时代的娱乐方式，动画总是最重要的娱乐方式之一。自 1995 年发布《玩具总动员》以来，迪士尼影业公司和皮克斯动画工作室已经发布了 12 个电脑动画长片，创下一共高达 4 亿美元的票房。

梦工厂出品的《史莱克》和其他电脑动画电影，如《冰河世纪》、《快乐的大脚》的成功表明了电脑动画在未来会挤掉传统的二维动画，成为占主导地位的动画形式。一直以来电脑主要是用来处理二维图形的。然而，随着技术的进步和软件程序功能的进步，电脑越来越多地被用来处理三维图形。

在不久的将来动画家们所面临的主要挑战之一是如何在电脑动画里描绘人类，毕竟大多数动画电影里的角色都是动物（《海底总动员》）或人格化的物体（《汽车总动员》）（实际情况是：一部动画电影从开始到完成平均需要四年的时间）。

当代动画家们面临的主要挑战在于他们制作真实人类的能力，包括所有的自然运动、生物力学，真实地再现自然生活的物理现象。众所周知要达到这种效果的难度是非常大的，在今天的动画产业里，能够给一个逼真的人类角色做动画被认为是最具挑战的事情。传统手绘动画就没有这个问题，在传统动画里艺术家对角色设计可以自由地尝试。

此外，电脑动画已经远远超出了家庭动画的范围，像《金刚》、《斯巴达》以及《蜘蛛侠》、《加勒比海盗》和《指环王》，从角色设计到物理模拟，这些电影制作的每一个方面都严重依赖电脑动画。当然，视频游戏也包含在电脑动画和图形设计里。

对于电脑动画常见的批评就是，制作动画只需要简单的技术训练就可以了，这样会彻底损害以故事为基础的手绘动画长片的发展。尽管最近电脑制作的动画电影大量涌现，但事实是，传统动画还远远没有结束。在2007年发布的二维动画《辛普森的一家》就是一个巨大的成功，成为迪士尼继2002年的《星际宝贝》之后最赚钱的动画电影。同时，迪士尼《魔法奇缘》（一个10分钟的手绘动画）的成功说明了二维动画依然有它的魅力。迪士尼也制作了自2004年以来的第一部传统二维动画《公主与青蛙》，该片以迪士尼的第一位黑人公主为重要角色，并于2009年12月上映。

Unit 2　Principles and Methods of Animation Creation
第 2 单元　动画创作的原理和方法

2.1　Basic Principles of Animation 1
动画片的基本原理（一）

Text

The following 12 basic principles of animation were developed by the "old men" of Walt Disney Studios during the 1930's. These principles came as a result of reflection about their practice and through Disney's desire to devise a way of animating that seemed more "real" in terms of how things moved, and how that movement might be used to express character and personality.

Squash and Stretch

By far the most important principle was what we call Squash and Stretch. You're probably familiar with this animation concept from Disney characters. They have a rubbery, elastic quality when they move. Animation is the art of exaggerating movement for dramatic and comic effect. The principles are simple: when an object hits something, it squashes and when it rises, it stretches. This is standard animation practice for 2D and much 3D. Just how much you exaggerate the effect will depend on the degree of realism you want to convey.

The standard animation test for all beginning artists was to draw a bouncing ball. Draw a ball, have it drop, hit the ground, and bounce back into the air. The harder the ground and the faster the velocity the ball contains before it hits the ground will define the amount of squash exerted on it. The amount of stretch is dependent on the degree of flexibility within the object being animated and the speed or velocity it is moving at.

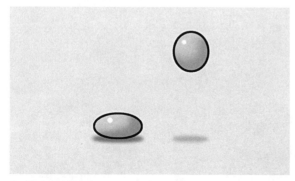

Application of squash and stretch for this ball.

If you freeze a movie sequence of a moving shape you will notice that it will actually appear as a blur. In animation, specifically drawn 2D animation, it is not easy to emulate the blur look. Consequently, the animator has to distort, or "stretch", the object to give the illusion of this fast-action blur.

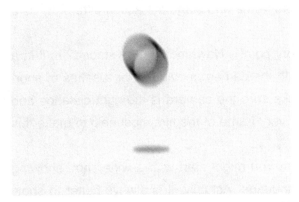

A simulated-motion blur effect to emulate the real-world appearance of a ball moving fast through space.

Anticipation

Most students know that for every action there is a subtle and opposite reaction, that's called Anticipation. Anticipation is used to better prepare the audience for a major action and to give more impact with the action being attempted.

Simply put, anticipation demands that if you have to animate a character's action in one particular direction, then you should first have a little back movement in the opposite direction to make it more dynamic. All actions can benefit from the use of anticipation. All actions need to have a little anticipation employed at their beginning to make the main action have a greater impact.

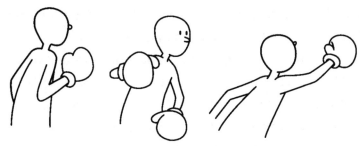

The middle of action is a backward anticipation position, then the impact of the punch will be so much the greater.

Anticipations can be as big as the broadest physical action or as small as a change of expression. For instance, the simple blink of an eye can be occasionally emphasized by the eye widening for a fraction a split-second before it closes. Few movements in real life occur without some kind of anticipation. It seems to be the natural way for creatures to move, and without it there would be little power in any action.

Staging

Staging is the filmic process of setting the scene and framing the shots to get the maximum impact or communication from the action. You would tend to frame and stage the action differently as a director, considering angles, framing and scene length.

The most important consideration is always the "story point". How should it be staged? Is it in a long shot or in a close-up? Is it better in a master shot with the camera moving in, or a series of short cuts to different objects? If you are staging an action, make sure the camera is the right distance and right height from the character to show what he is doing. Every frame of the film must help to make this point of the story.

For example, if two persons are talking to each other, you might start with a wide shot, showing them both together and highlighting the particular body language. Actually, it is always better to show the action in silhouette, so that everything can be seen clearly. This means that you need to create clearly defined outlines to their poses. As long as the audience can clearly see what you want them to see, you will have succeeded in the staging and composition. Next, you could show the mood and reaction of them. So cut to the one who is still speaking, and then the one who is listening. Lastly, return to the wide shot to reveal the conclusion of the scene. Make sure the full-body action is well animated. In each of these framings you are effectively painting a picture with your camera as well as with your staging, so think every shot through and communicate it to your audience in the most significant way possible.

Straight Ahead Action and Pose to Pose

There are two main approaches to animation. The natural way is called Straight Ahead. Straight Ahead action starts at one point and finish at another in a single continuous movement. The planned way is called Pose to Pose. Here, the animator plans his action, put in the keys first, then find the nicest transition between two poses, make clear charts for assistant to draw the inbetweens.

When using Straight Ahead, we could get a natural flow of fluid and both the drawings and the action have a fresh, slightly zany look, as the animator keeps the whole process very creative. But we can tend to miss the point of the shot, time stretches and the shot gets longer and longer. Even characters grow and shrink. Pose to Pose is structured, calculated, and logical. It's a quick way to work and frees us up to do more scenes. But the action can be a bit choppy, and a bit unnatural.

Both methods are still in use because they each offer certain advantages for different types of action. Usually the best way is going to be the combination of Straight Ahead and Pose to Pose. First we roughly depict the character's probable progress. Then we make the keys, put in the extremes. Now we have the structure, work straight ahead on top of these guideposts. We may have to change and revise parts of the keys and extremes as we go along. Sometime when you don't know what to do in an action, just go straight ahead, start on ones.

Follow through and Overlapping Action

Follow through is the opposite of anticipation. When a character stops, the parts of the body don't come to a stop all at once, there's one part starts first such as the head, then a few frames later, the rest of the parts would settle into their final position, possibly not all at the same time, various parts of the body overlap each other, such as hair or clothes. This is easy to see in real life. The movement of each part must be timed carefully so it will have the correct feeling of weight. Overlapping Action is where the Follow through of one action becomes the anticipation of the next one.

So to make even the dullest action or figure interesting, we break the body into different entities and move sections, use the Follow through on the fleshy parts to give us the solidity and dimension, constantly overlapping. We could drag the parts to give the added feeling of weight and reality, and we could strengthen our poses for more vitality. All these added up to more life in the scene. The magic was beginning to appear.

Slow in and Slow out

Most moving objects don't begin and end the movement at full speed. They begin slowly, get up to speed and slow down before drawing to a stop. Think of a car starting, driving and stopping. Because this smooth, slow in/slow out type of movement is so common. In 2D animation, this means putting more inbetweens close to each extreme at the beginning and end of an action and fewer in the middle. This creates a more lifelike feeling to the movement.

You might not want this type of movement when you need the movement to be sharper, for example when lid falls shut from an open position, when the ball hitting the ground. When work 3D animation, discriminate use of software's default slow in/slow out motion gives an unnatural, floating look, so use appropriately and with due care.

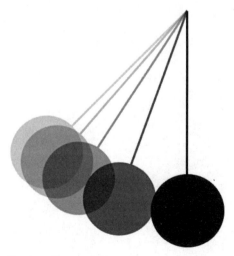

See how the pendulum swings.

Inbetween slow-ins and slow-outs needs a little more focus when placing and approaching the sequence of inbetweens to be attempted. With the chart in the following figure, notice that the first inbetween drawing between 1 and 9 is drawing 7. With drawing 7 done, drawing 5 is the next inbetween position between drawings 1 and 7. Finally, with drawing 5 done, drawing 3 has to be completed between 1 and 5.

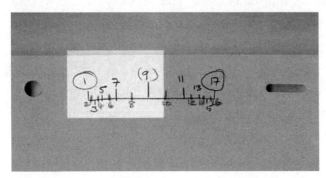

Notice the inbetween drawings.

Similarly when approaching the slow out part of the chart. This should give you a complete accelerating/decelerating swing to the pendulum.

Words and phrases

  dramatic 戏剧的
  bouncing 跳跃的，弹起的
  velocity 速度，速率
  blur 模糊不清
  dynamic 动态，动力，动力学的，有活力的
  filmic 电影的，像电影的
  approach 方法，途径，接近
  inbetween 中间画，中间帧
  logical 合逻辑的，合理的
  accelerate 增速，使加快
  decelerate 减速
  basic principles of animation 动画的基本原理
  squash and stretch 挤压和拉伸
  anticipation 预备动作
  staging 布局，表演
  long shot 远景镜头
  close-up 特写镜头
  wide shot 全景镜头
  reveal the conclusion 揭示结论

straight ahead　逐帧，连续动作画法
pose to pose　关键帧画法
ones　一拍一
follow through　跟随动作
overlapping action　重叠动作
slow in　慢入，渐入
slow out　慢出，渐出
discriminate use of　区别使用
chart　运动标尺

Practice

1. Draw a bouncing ball for practice, use the most important principle called Squash and Stretch.

2. Create a generic walk cycle on one's, note Follow through and Overlapping Action of each part.

3. Straight Ahead Action and Pose to Pose are the main approaches to animation, indicate the difference between them.

Translate into English

1. 在每个动作发生之前有一个细微的方向相反的动作，这就是预备动作，预备动作用来使观众为主要动作做好准备以及给予动作更强的力度。

2. 在动画开始之前，你应该像电影导演那样设计每一个镜头，要考虑拍摄的角度、镜头构图和拍摄时间等问题。

Further reading

The Illusion of Life: Disney Animation
Editor: Frank Thomas, Ollie Johnston, Johnson
Publisher: Hyperion (1995)

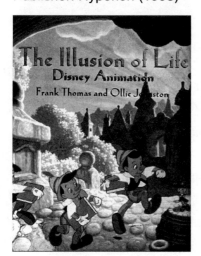

Web links

www.disneyanimation.com

Translation of text

以下的12项动画基本原则是1930年代华特·迪士尼工作室的前辈们总结出来的。这些原则来自于他们的工作经验，以及迪士尼对动画的本质和如何表现角色个性的探索。

压缩与拉长

最重要的基本原则就是压缩和拉长。你可以通过迪士尼的动画角色来了解这个概念。当他们有动作时都会看起来有弹性、很灵活。动画是一种通过夸大动作来达到戏剧和漫画效果的艺术。这条原则很简单：当物体发生碰撞时要挤压，当物体上升时要拉长。这是很多二维和三维动画的绘制准则。至于挤压拉长到什么程度取决于你想表现的是现实风格还是卡通风格。

对新手来说最基本的练习是画一个弹跳的小球。画一个球，让它下落，撞到地面，弹回到空中。地面越硬球速越快，这也决定了小球挤压的程度。拉长程度则取决于物体的灵活性和它移动的速度。

如果你将一部电影暂停，你会发现正在运动的物体实际上是模糊的状态。在动画里，尤其是二维动画，不太容易画出这个模糊的瞬间。因此，动画师们不得不将物体变形或者拉长使其呈现出高速运动的假象。

预备动作

大多数学生知道每个动作之前有一个细微的方向相反的动作，这叫做预备动作。预备动作用来使观众为主要动作做好准备以及给予动作更强的冲击力。

简单地说，预备动作的要求是如果你要在一个特定方向上画一个角色的动作，应该首先在反方向上有一个细微的退后动作来使它更加逼真。使用预备动作可以让所有的动作都有更好的效果。在所有动作开始的时候加入预备动作可以使主要动作更有力度。

预备动作能够大到肢体动作，也可以小到细微的表情变化。例如，强调眨眼动作可以通过眼睛闭上前的瞬间睁大动作来实现。现实生活中的运动发生时几乎都有预备动作。加入预备动作可以让动作看上去更自然、更有力量。

表演布局

和拍电影一样，动画也需要这样一个设置场景及设计镜头的过程，并从角色动作中得到最强烈的表达效果。你应该像电影导演那样设计镜头，安排每一个动作，考虑拍摄的角度、镜头构图和拍摄时间。

要考虑的最重要的因素永远都是故事点。应该怎么布局？远景还是近景？是用主观镜头推进更好，还是对一组不同物体的快切更好？如果你拍摄一个镜头，为了更好地展示角色动作，摄像机要安排在一个合适的距离和位置。影片的每个镜头的构图和设计必须有助于故事点。

例如，如果两个人在交谈，你可以以一个全景镜头开始，显示他俩在一起，强调他们不同的身体语言。实际上，用剪影的形式更好一些，因为这样所有的细节都会被看清楚。这意味着你需要给角色姿态绘制清晰的轮廓线。只要观众能够清楚地看到你想给他们看到的东西，你就在构图布局上成功了。接着，你应该表现他们之间的情绪和反应。所以应该切到其中正在说话的那个人的特写，然后是另一个人的特写。最后，回到全景镜头来揭示这个场景的结论。要确保全身的动作都被很好地绘制出来。在每一帧镜头里，像用摄像机一样用设计布局来呈现画面，所以要考虑如何用最有效的方式通过镜头把想法传递给观众。

连续动作与关键动作

做动画有两个主要的方法。自然的方式叫连续动作法。连续动作在一个单独持续的动作中从一点开始一直画到结束。计划的方式叫关键动作法。动画师要给动作作计划，先画一些关键帧，然后画两个姿势间的过渡，做出运动标尺来帮助助手添加中间画。

使用连续动作法，我们可以得到一个非常自然的绘制流程，图画和动作看起来都会很新颖、略微有点奇怪，同时动画师要保持整个过程具有创造性。但是这样也可能无法把握住镜头的关键点，时间拉长了，镜头会很拖沓，甚至角色会变形。关键动作法是结构化的，是计算过的、逻辑化的。它快速有效，可以节省很多时间。但是缺点是角色动作可能有点起伏，不太自然。

两个方法都可以用，因为在不同类型的动作中它们各有所长。通常最好的方式是混合使用两种方法。首先，我们粗略地描绘角色的行动过程，然后加入关键帧和原画。现在我们得到了主要的结构，在这些结构的参考下用连续动作法继续绘制。在绘制过程中我们可能需要修改一部分关键帧和原画。当你不知道怎么设计动作时，也可以用连续动作法，用一拍一来尝试。

跟随动作与重叠动作

跟随动作是和预备动作相对的。当一个角色停下时，身体的各个部分不会全部都立刻停下，身体某部分先动，比如头，几帧后，其余部分进到它们的最终位置，但是也不会在同一时间，身体不同部分会彼此重叠，比如身体和衣服。这样的例子在生活中很常见。动作的每个部分的时间都必须仔细计算好，这样才能呈现出正确的重量感。重叠动作是一个动作的跟随动作变成下一个跟随动作的预备动作。

因此，为了使迟钝的动作或者角色变得更有趣，我们把身体分成不同的实体和运动单元，在肉多的部分使用跟随动作来呈现体积感，不断地重叠。我们可拖拽一部分来呈现重量感和真实感，并且我们还可加强姿势来表现活力。所有这些将会给场景增添更多的生活元素，效果会非常好。

慢入与慢出

大部分物体在开始或结束的时候不会全速移动。开始时很慢，速度逐渐加快，在结束前开始降速。想象一辆车的启动、行驶和停车就是这样。因为这种平滑、渐进渐出型的运动非常普遍。在二维动画里，这就意味着一个动作在接近起始和结束位置的原画中间加入更多的中间画，相应在中间减少。这就创造出了更有真实感的动作。

当你画一个敏捷的动作时，你不需要用这种方法。例如，盖上盖子，球撞击地面。当我们做三维动画时，要注意的是使用软件默认的慢入慢出功能会出现不自然的效果，所以要注意合理使用。

在给慢进慢出加中间画时需要注意多反复尝试。图中是一个慢进慢出的运动标尺，注意第一个中间画要加在 1 和 9 之间，标做 7。接着是在 1 和 7 之间加入中间画 5。最后，在 1 和 5 之间加入中间画 3。

用同样的方法制作标尺慢出的部分，这样我们就得到了一个速度加减的钟摆。

2.2 Basic Principles of Animation 2
动画片的基本原理（二）

Text

Arcs and Paths of Action

Nothing in life moves in a perfectly straight line. Everything moves in curves or arcs. Some actions create circular movements because they usually pivot around a central point, usually a joint. Consequently, you have to remember this whenever you are animating anything. Arcs are used to describe natural movement.

Now that you have seen the pendulum successfully swing from side to side. You can see the principle best if you mark the center of the pendulum ball on every one of the drawings one by one. You will end up with a series of positions that are in an arc.

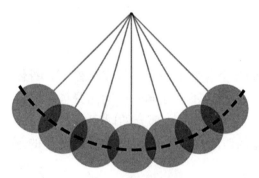

The arc that is described by the center of the pendulum's head as it swings backward and forward.

This arc can also be described as the path of action of the swinging pendulum ball, a term that animators use to describe the central, core movement in any animated action figure.

The path of action or the arc of any movement is something that should never be forgotten by any animator, whether they are creating key poses or simply putting in inbetweens for any extended movement.

As this principle is better understood, we plan out the scenes with rough poses, as well as the key actions, determine how high and how low the character should go in any action. Then sketch in the arcs, to guide the eventual drawings along this curved path.

Secondary Action

Secondary action is just that, another action that takes place at the same time as the main one. This may be something as simple as turning the head from side to side during a walk sequence. Adding secondary actions to the main action gives a scene more life, and can help to support the main action.

Secondary action creates interest and realism in animation. But the important thing is that it should be staged such that it can be noticed but still not overpower the main action. In the case of facial expressions, expression change must come before the move, or after. A change in the middle of a major move will go unnoticed, and any value intended will be lost.

First we animate the most important move. Then we go through the scene a second time animating the secondary action. Then continue to change and adjust until all parts of the drawing work together in a very natural way. All of these actions should work together in support of one another.

Timing and Weight

Timing is the essence of animation. The speed at which something moves gives a sense of what the object is, the weight of an object, and why it is moving. The personalities that are developing more by their movements, and the varying speed of those movements determine whether the character is lethargic, excited, nervous, relaxed. Neither acting nor attitude could be portrayed without paying very close attention to timing.

Use this principle to enhance the quality of animation, that by executing the action by including the elements of weight and gravity. One of the biggest failings of inexperienced animators is their inability to create a sense of weight in their work. Weight defines character, personality, and gravity in a scene. However, poor-quality animation often fails to communicate this.

The illusion of weight in animation starts with the key poses you give your character. For example, here are two illustrations of a character holding a weight. The reason the second drawing looks like the character really is carrying a heavy weight is because his pose and posture support it.

Note that on the heavier pose the character's legs are bent to support the weight, and he is also leaning backward to counter the additional weight at the front of his body.

Here are a few tips that will help you create weight in your animation:

1. When posing a character who is dealing with weight, remember that the strongest parts of the human body are the legs.

2. The heavier an object is, the slower it moves or can be moved.

3. Using Slow Out chart timing for the initial raising of the weight.

4. If a character has a heavy build, or at least has a certain amount of weight around his or her stomach, butt, or breasts, remember to employ some overlapping action on these areas.

5. Because of gravity, characters who carrying weight will always suggest downward sag to their pose.

Exaggeration

Exaggeration is an effect especially useful for animation, as perfect imitation of reality can look static and dull in cartoons. It is not extreme distortion of a drawing or extremely broad, violent action all the time. It should be used in a careful and balanced manner, not arbitrarily.

The level of exaggeration depends on whether one seeks realism or a particular style. In feature animation, a character must move more broadly to look natural, but the action should not be as broad as in a short cartoon style. It is important to employ a certain level of restraint when using exaggeration; if a scene contains several elements, there should be a balance in how those elements are exaggerated in relation to each other, to avoid confusing or overawing the viewer. Exaggeration in a walk or an eye movement or even a head turn will give your film more appeal.

Solid Drawing

The principle of solid drawing means taking into account forms in three-dimensional space, giving them volume, depth and weight. The animator needs to be a skilled draughtsman and has to understand the basics of three-dimensional shapes, anatomy, weight, balance, light and shadow, etc..

When work animation, you draw in the classical sense, using pencil sketches and drawings for reproduction of life. Then you transform these line works into color and movement giving the characters the illusion of three-dimensional life. You'll have to draw the character in all positions and from every angle. If you can't do it, and have to stage it from some other angle, it's very restrictive and takes longer.

Modern-day computer animators draw less because of the facilities computers give them, yet their work benefits greatly from a basic understanding of animation principles and their additions to basic computer animation.

Appeal

The animated drawings should have appeal. This is giving personality to the characters you draw. If you can convey appeal without the sound track, you know you are on the right track.

A weak drawing lacks appeal. Poor design, clumsy shapes, awkward moves, all these are low on appeal. Appeal can be gained by correctly utilizing other principles such as exaggeration in design, avoiding symmetry, using overlapping action, and others.

It's important to note that appeal doesn't necessarily mean good vs. evil. All characters have to have appeal whether they are heroic, villainous, comic or cute. Appeal, as you will use it, includes an easy to read design, clear drawing, and personality development that will capture and involve the audience's interest. For example, in Disney's animated classic "Peter Pan", Captain Hook is an evil character, but most people would agree that his character and design has appeal. The same goes for Hopper in "A Bug's Life". Even though he's mean and nasty, his design and characterization/personality still has a lot of appeal.

Personality

This word isn't actually a true principle of animation, but refers to the correct application of the other principles. Personality determines the success of an animation. The idea is that the animated creature really becomes alive and enters the true character of the role. One character would not perform an action the same way in two different emotional states. No two characters would act the same. It is also important to make the personality of a character distinct, but at the same time be familiar to the audience. Personality has a lot to do with what is going on in the mind of the character, as well as the traits and mannerisms of the character. It is helpful to have some background in acting, and certainly taking acting or improve class as an animator is a good idea.

Words and phrases

curves   曲线
arc   弧线，圆弧
circular   圆形的，循环的
pivot   枢轴，中心点
pendulum   钟摆，摇锤
personality   个性，性格
portray   描绘，扮演
gravity   重力，地心引力
poor-quality   质量差的，品质低劣的
sketch   素描，写生，草图
restrictive   限制的，约束的
symmetry   对称，整齐，匀称
trait   特性，特质，性格
secondary action   二级动作
timing and weight   时间控制和重量
exaggeration   夸张
solid drawing   实体描绘
three-dimensional space   三维空间
appeal   吸引力
sound track   声道，声轨
peter pan   《小飞侠》，迪士尼于1953年出品的第14部经典动画，长篇剧情动画片。
a bug's Life   《虫虫危机》，博伟国际于1998年出品的三维动画长片。

Practice

1. Taking a three-quarter view of a horse, create a cycle of it walking eccentrically.
2. Demonstrate how you can execute a character action that communicates a greater sense of weight.
3. With a character of your own design, animate a basketball player taking a penalty shot.

Translate into English

1. 不论是绘制关键帧还是中间画,动画师都要牢牢记住任何运动都有行动路径。
2. 夸张的程度取决于你想要的动画风格。
3. 能否塑造个性是一个角色是否成功的关键。

Further reading

Animation: The Mechanics of Motion
Editor: Chris Webster
Publisher: Focal Press (2005)

Web links

www.animationarena.com

Translation of text

弧线与运动轨迹

现实中没有物体是沿着绝对的直线运动的。所有物体的运动轨迹都是曲线或者弧线。有些动作是圆周运动,因为它们通常围绕一个中心点转动,比如骨骼关节。因此,你要记住给任何物体做动画都要遵循这条原则,要用弧线来描述运动轨迹。

现在你看到钟摆从一边摇摆到另一边。如果你对每一个摆球的中心作标记，就会得到一个由一系列点组成的弧形，这样你就可以很好地理解这条原则。

这条弧线也可以理解成摆球的运动路径，这种方法经常用在动画角色身上。

不论是绘制关键帧还是中间画，动画师都要牢牢记住任何运动都有行动路径或弧形轨迹。

要更好地理解这一原则，我们先规划出动作的草图，接着是关键动作，决定角色每个动作的位置。然后绘制出运动轨迹，最后沿着这条曲线来绘制每一张图画。

二级动作

二级动作就是和主要动作同时发生的动作。就像走路的同时转动头部。在主要动作的基础上加入二级动作会感觉更真实自然，可以帮助更好地表现主要动作。

二级动作可以给动画增添趣味和真实感。但最重要的是，它应该被好好安排，它既要被注意到，但又不能喧宾夺主。在绘制面部表情的时候，表情变化要安排在行动之前或之后。在行动中间安排一个细节将不会被注意到，也达不到预想的效果。

首先我们绘制动画的主要动作。然后我们从头检查一遍并加入二级动作。接着继续修改和调整直到所有的部分都很协调。

时间控制和重量

时间是动画的精髓。物体移动的速度会表现出物体的质感、重量和运动的原因。物体的运动状态可以表现出它的个性，不同的运动速度可以决定角色的状态是否是慵懒的、兴奋的、紧张的，还是轻松的。无论是表演还是状态都要依靠时间控制来表现。

利用这一原理，可以通过加入重量和重力的元素来提高动画的质量。没有经验的动画师最大的缺点之一就是无法表现重量感。在一个场景中重量定义了角色特点、个性和重力感。然而，劣质的动画没有办法表达出这些。

表现物体重量要从角色的关键姿势开始。例如，这里有两个人抬着同样的重物。第二个人看起来真的是抬着很重的东西，这是因为他的姿势和姿态表现出了重量感。

以下是在动画中表现重量感的几个技巧：

1. 当表现一个人负重的时候，要记住动作最夸张的部位是双腿。
2. 越重的物体，移动的速度越慢。
3. 用慢出的运动标尺来表现重物的提速。
4. 如果一个角色很胖，记得要在肚子、屁股、胸部这些部位加入重叠动作来表现重量感。
5. 因为存在重力，所以角色在搬运重物时在姿态上会有下垂的状态。

夸张

夸张是一种特别适用于动画的表现效果，可以完美地模仿现实中看起来是静止的以及很沉闷的角色。这不需要在形体上极度扭曲或者一直保持猛烈的动作。用这个技法的时候要谨慎要平衡，不能太随意。

夸张的程度取决于是寻求现实主义还是一种特定的风格。在动画电影中，角色的动作幅度必须更大一些看起来才自然，但动作幅度不应该和卡通风格的动画短片一样。运用夸张手法时最重要的是要约束夸张的程度，如果一个场景中包含几个元素，这些元素夸张的程度要彼此平衡，以避免让观众混淆。在走路、眼睛动作甚至是转头时用夸张的手法可以使动画更有吸引力。

实体描绘

实体描绘这一原则就是加入体积感、深度和重量感，赋予图画三维立体空间的感觉。动画师要有熟练的绘制技巧，要了解三维立体物体的形态、结构、重量、平衡、光线和阴影等的基本原理。

做动画的时候，通常先用传统的方法来绘制，用铅笔稿来再现生活场景。然后将这些线条转化成色彩稿并且动起来，以此来给角色创造出一个三维立体的生活空间。你必须先从各种位置和角度来绘制出大量的角色形态，这样可以直接用在每个镜头里，最大限度地节省时间。

现如今的电脑动画师绘制得较少，因为电脑可以帮助他们完成很多工作，这得益于他们很好地掌握了动画原理并将其应用在电脑动画上。

吸引力

动画应该是有吸引力的。通过一张张的图画来赋予角色鲜活的个性。如果在没有音响效果的情况下你可以传达出吸引力，这说明你真的成功了。

劣质的设计，笨拙的形状和动作，这些都无法让角色具有吸引力。正确地使用如夸张等各种动画原理和技法，避免相同的动作，使用重叠动作，可以增加角色的魅力。

有一点要注意，吸引力并不一定意味着只有好人有，而坏的角色没有。所有的角色都应该有魅力，不论它是英勇的、邪恶的、滑稽的还是可爱的。要实现角色的魅力就要有直观的设计、清晰的画风，以及能吸引观众的角色个性。例如，迪士尼的经典动画《小飞侠》里有个角色是虎克船长，他是一个坏人，但是很多人都认为他的性格塑造以及形象设计都很棒。《虫虫危机》里的跳虫也是一样，虽然它很卑鄙，但是它的形象设计和个性塑造让人印象深刻。

个性

这一条不能算动画原理，而是指其他原理的正确应用。性格塑造决定了一个动画是否成功。这个概念是指如何让动画角色真的鲜活起来。一个角色在不同的情绪情景下表演同一个动作，会用到不一样的表现方式。两个角色永远不会有一样的表演。角色的个性鲜明很重要，但是也要让观众很容易接受。角色的内心世界是什么样的，表现出来的性格以及言谈举止就是什么样的。背景和情景设定有助于角色的表演，参加一些表演课程来提高专业素质对动画师来说是一个好主意。

2.3　The Production Process of 2D Animation

二维动画的创作流程

Text

The production process is slightly different at different studios around the world. However, because of the demands of the medium, there are similarities, and we can generalize. Therefore, the production process follows in a general way.

Script

Usually animation begins with a script. If there is no script, then there is at least some kind of idea in written form—an outline or treatment.

Voice Recording

Sound can be a huge factor in an animated production. Without great voices, even the best animation will seem flat and uninteresting. When filmmaking, it is always best to record your soundtrack elements professionally. If you are using dialog in your work, you will definitely need some kind of sound breakdown technology.

Storyboard

Storyboard artists take the script and create the first visualization of the story. Often these boards are still a little rough. In projects each major action and major pose is drawn within a frame. The dialogue and action are listed underneath each frame.

Animatic

Once we have finalized our storyboards, we need to get a good feel for the flow of the story before we start animating. To do this we time the scenes and create an animatic, which is an animated video of the storyboards. Animatics can also get as fancy as productions want them to be, including moving elements, pans, zooms, and more.

Character and Prop Design

Once the animatic has been approved, it and the storyboards are sent to the design departments. Art director and character designers prepare model sheets for all important characters and props in the film. These model sheets will show how a character or object looks from a variety of angles with a variety of poses and expressions, so that all artists working on the project can deliver consistent work.

Background Design

Background artists are responsible for all location designs. The designer will design these line drawings from the roughs done by the storyboard artist. Then a background painter will paint a few key backgrounds for establishing shots. Background artists usually paint in the traditional way, but some or all elements can be painted digitally.

Layout

The design of the layouts comes either from the production illustrations, or from the storyboards. Layout artists further refine each shot, setting camera angles and movements, composition, staging, and lighting. Sometime layout may be skipped, basically, by doing detailed drawings at the storyboard stage. Later these can be blown up to the correct size.

X-Sheet

The director or animators fill out X-sheet (Dope Sheets), using the information found on the audio track. These sheets will be a template or blueprint for the production, frame by frame and layer by layer.

Animation

The animator receives the dialogue track of his section of the story, the model sheets, copies of the layouts, and X-Sheets. There are boxes on the X-sheets for the animator to fill in with the details, layer by layer, as the animation is being planned. Animation paper has a series of holes for pegs so that it can be lined up correctly for a camera.

Animators use pencil tests to test the animation. Constant testing of scenes as they are being drawn helps the animator make timing and acting adjustments.

Clean-up artists or assistant animators clean up the rough animation poses drawn by the animator and sketch the key action in between. A breakdown artist or inbetweener may be responsible for the easier poses between those. Visual effects animators animate elements like fire, water, and props.

Scanning

The quality of your scans will make a huge difference in the final quality of your digital cels. The threshold, darkness, or contrast settings are important.

Color

Color stylists set the color palette for a show. It's important that they choose colors that not only look good together but that will make the characters stand out from the background. Different palettes may be needed for different lighting conditions.

Post-Production and Editing

The compositors take all the backgrounds, characters, props, and effects and seamlessly blend them together with the proper camera moves. The editor takes all the composited scenes and dialogue and edits them together in the proper sequence, transitions are added. The sound designer builds and adds the sound effects and balances the music, voice, and effects so that all are easily heard and understood. Sometimes a film is generated, and it must be color corrected. The directors, producers view the completed work. Notes are given, changes are made, and retakes are done. Final approvals are given, and a release print is made. The completed project is now ready for delivery.

Equipment and Tools

Two-Dimensional Animation Lightbox

Lightboxes can come in all shapes and sizes. A good animator's lightbox, however, will ideally have an adjustable working surface, so that that animator can find the best angles to comfortably draw anything. The crucial thing about any animator's work surface, however, is that it has to be composed of some kind of translucent material that enables a backlight to shine through several layers of animation paper at a time.

Peg Bar

All animation paper is punched with holes that ensure perfect registration from drawing to drawing. The peg bar is the means by which these punched sheets of animation paper can be kept in perfect alignment with one another as they are being worked on upon the lightbox surface.

Animation Paper

There are just a few different types of animation paper. Some are thinner, and others are sturdier. We should use a combination of them. We use the thin paper for rough animation and the thicker, more expensive paper for clean-up.

Animation Pencils

Pretty much all pencils will work for animation, but there are ones that are preferred by most animators. Red and blue pencils are quite often used for the rough and clean-up stages of work. Mechanical pencils are usually the preferred pencil to cleaned-up drawings, as the black line is appropriate for scanner copying and digital coloring.

Field Guide

Although the above equipment enables animators to work, they do need to define a required area to work in. Consequently, transparent plastic field guides are required to identify the "field" that the animation is to be seen in.

X-sheet

The key administrative paperwork that 2D animators specifically will need is a pad of X-sheets. X-sheets (dope sheet) are crucial to animators who are organizing their thoughts and plotting their movements and layers.

Technology Requirements

When you finish a sequence of action, the drawings need to be filmed and played back for inspection and critique. This is universally known as a pencil test. Consequently, you will need some kind of image-capture device and software that will allow you to do this.

Scanners

Once an animation is pencil tested and approved, it will need to be cleaned up and taken to the next level. Here, each individual drawing will be scanned as individual files. To initiate this process, you will obviously need a suitable flatbed scanner.

Words and phrases

visualization　可视化，视觉化
refine　精炼，提纯，改善
blueprint　蓝图，设计图，计划
threshold　临界值，阈值，入口，开始
darkness　暗色，明度
contrast　对比度
translucent　透亮的，半透明的
alignment　对齐，对准
script　脚本，剧本
voice recording　声音录制
storyboard　故事板，分镜头
animatic　动态分镜
pan　摇镜头，平移
zoom　缩放，变焦
model sheet　人物设计，模型表
art director　艺术指导，艺术总监
blow up　吹胀，放大
pencil test　铅笔稿测试
clean-up　清稿
inbetweener　中间画画手
color stylist　色彩风格师
color palette　调色板
post-production　后期制作
seamlessly blend　无缝地融合
editor　剪辑师
sound designer　音响设计师
director　导演
producer　制片人
lightbox　灯箱
field guide　规格框
X-sheet　摄影表
image-capture device　图像捕捉设备

Practice

1. Review and summarize the general production process of 2D animation.
2. What's peg bar? And how to use it?

Translate into English

1. 动画创作通常都是从剧本开始的。
2. 动态分镜就是一个视频版的故事板，包括画面、镜头的推、拉、摇、移和音响效果等。

Further reading

Producing Independent 2D Character Animation: Making and Selling a Short Film
Editor: Mark Simon
Publisher: Focal Press (2003)

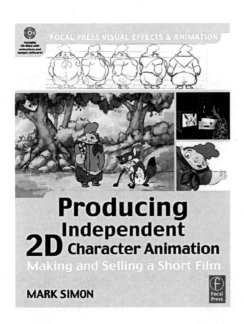

Web links

www.2danimationstudio.com

Translation of text

不同的动画工作室工作方法也不一样。因为动画这一媒介的特殊要求，工作方法都有相似之处，我们可以总结出来。所以，创作过程大致如下。

脚本

通常每部动画都是从脚本开始。如果没有，也至少应该有文字形式的想法——即故事梗概或者情节大纲。

声音录制

在动画片里声音是一个非常重要的元素。没有完美的声音，即使再好的动画也会看起来平淡无味。当制作动画时，通常最好用专业的方法来录制音频。如果在片子里使用对话，就需要有音频剪辑技术。

故事板

故事板艺术家用脚本绘制出第一个可视化版本。通常这些故事板画得比较简略。镜头里的每个关键动作和主要姿态都要画在指定的镜头框里。对白和动作被要求写在镜头框下面。

动态分镜头

完成故事板之后，在制作动画之前，我们需要对故事的整体效果有个了解。将所有的镜头剪辑好制作成一个动态分镜头，也就是一个视频版的故事板。动态分镜头可以像动画片的完成品那样有丰富的视听效果，包含镜头的推、拉、摇、移等。

角色和道具设计

动态分镜头通过后，将和故事板一起移交到设计部门。艺术指导和角色设计师要给所有角色和道具绘制造型模板。这些模板要展示角色和物品的各个角度，各种姿势和表情，这样所有的工作人员的画稿将会保持一致。

背景设计

背景画师要负责所有场景的绘制。背景设计师根据故事板草稿来设计并画出线稿。背景画师给确定下来的镜头背景上色。他们通常用传统方法手绘背景，当然也可以一部分或者全部都用电脑绘制。

构图

构图设计可以参考动画概念稿和故事板。构图设计师进一步细化每一个镜头，设置摄影机的角度和运动、镜头组成、表演布局以及光影。有时候这个步骤可以省略，直接在故事板阶段将细致的构图画好，之后扩成放大稿。

摄影表

导演或者动画师参考音轨给出的信息来填写摄影表。这些摄影表逐帧逐层，将是动画片的模板或蓝图。

做动画

动画师收到动画片段的音轨、角色模板、背景构图和摄影表。摄影表需要动画师逐帧逐层的填写，动画就是这样被安排的。有孔洞的动画定位纸与定位尺一起使用，这样一组镜头就都是对齐的。

动画师用铅笔稿测试来检查动作。这样有助于动画师做时间和动作上的调整和修改。清稿工作人员或者助理动画师来给动画师粗略的动画姿势做清稿以及画出中间的关键动作。中间画师将负责原画之间的简单过渡。视觉效果动画师将绘制其他元素，例如火、水和道具。

扫描

扫描的质量直接决定了影片最终的质量。扫描时的阈值、明度或对比度设置很重要。

上色

上色师给片子设置色板。重要的是他们选择颜色不但为了好看同时也为了背景能把角色衬托得更突出。针对不同的光照情况应该设计出几套不同的色板。

后期制作和剪辑

合成师将所有的背景、角色、道具、特效用适当的摄影机运动合成到一起。剪辑师将所有合成好的镜头、对话按照适当的顺序编辑好，加入转场。音效师制作并加入音效，并且调整音乐、对白、音效，这样所有的声音都会被听懂。有时候影片生成了，还需要校色。导演和制片人观看完成的片子，给出意见，做调整，重新制作。最后检验通过，制作出准许上映的版本。这样完成的动画片就可以发行了。

设备和工具

二维动画灯箱

灯箱可以是任何大小任何形状的。灯箱要有一个可调节的工作面，这样动画师就可以找到最舒服的角度来画各种东西。对于工作面来说最关键的是材质必须是半透明的，这样背景灯才能穿透好几层动画定位纸。

动画定位尺

所有的动画定位纸都打有孔洞，这样每张图画才能保持对齐。定位尺的功能就是将定位纸对齐并固定在灯箱工作面上。

动画定位纸

定位纸有厚薄之分。做动画时要根据情况来选择。薄的可以用来画草稿，比较贵的厚纸可以用来清稿。

动画铅笔

做动画会用到很多铅笔，其中有些大部分动画师都特别偏爱。红色和蓝色彩铅经常在草稿和清稿阶段使用。自动铅笔通常用来画最终的线稿，因为均匀的黑色线条很适合扫描仪以及电脑上色。

规格框

虽然以上提到的设备和工具能用来做动画，但是动画师还需要一个工具来确定画面尺寸。透明塑料的规格框就是用来定义镜头规格的。

摄影表

二维动画师要重点处理的文书工作就是填写一堆摄影表。摄影表用来实现动画师的想法以及来分层安排动作节奏。

技术要求

当你完成一组动作后,需要将它们拍摄下来并且反复回放,以此来检查和修改。这就是铅笔稿测试。因此你需要图像捕捉设备和相应的软件。

扫描仪

当一组动画已经做过铅笔稿测试并且检验通过,就可以清稿并进行下一步工作。每一张图画都要扫描成一个单独的文件。要完成这项工作你需要一个合适的平板扫描仪。

2.4 The Process of 3D Animation
三维动画的创作流程

Text

Because the computing power is now available to anyone, we are likely to see a continuing growth in 3D animated films. But, it's all about the story. That's why Pixar's films work, not because of the fantastic rendering software, or the way they get fur to move, but because the stories and the characters are great.

3D animation is produced differently from 2D, but the processes of pre-production and post-production are usually the same, such as script, storyboard, character design, etc. This chapter takes you through the basics of 3D animation using affordable software.

Equipment

Pretty much everyone has access to a good computer these days, but you should be aware that the programs you'll need for 3D animation will need a significant amount of RAM storage and a large hard drive to contain the inevitably large files that animation movie files require. Nowadays, many powerful workstation computers are used instead of home computer. Graphics workstation computers use two to four processors, and thus are a lot more powerful than a home computer, and are specialized for rendering. A large number of workstations (known as a Render Farm) are networked together to effectively act as a giant computer. The more expensive stations are able to render much faster, due to the more technologically advanced hardware that they contain.

Software

One of the factors that will affect your decision is the type of animation you want to tackle. The top-end commercial software packages, such as Maya, 3Ds Max are very complex programs that can handle everything. Now both brands are actually owned by Autodesk (www.autodesk.com), and the gaps between them are beginning to narrow.

Modeling

Designs are usually created in 2D first, approved, and sent for modeling in 3D. Characters can be modeled on a computer, often from basic geometric shapes, and the parts fused, or sculptures can be digitized as a wire-frame model. Most 3D program divide the screen into four separate camera views so that you can clearly see what is happening to your object as you manipulate it.

In 3D animation, although you don't have to create every frame of action, you do have to build every object that appears in the film. At this stage, you also need to build up your scenes, not only interiors but also exteriors, including locations, sets, props and environments, etc. The more realistic you want it, the more you have to build.

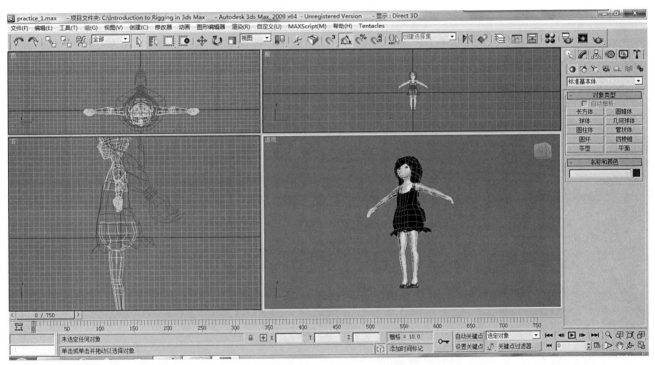

Character modeling (created in Max).

Shaders and Textures

Shaders and textures are a vital part of the 3D process, as they provide a realistic look to the object's surfaces.

Shaders control a surface's overall appearance, most shading is divided into seven distinct areas: color, highlight and shininess, bump, reflection, transparency, refraction and glow. These can be applied individually or mixed together to create the desired effect. Each program has its own method for handling this function, but, as with modelling, the basic theory is the same.

Depending on the different effect, you also need to use texture maps, they are the images that are placed on a surface. These images are usually created in an external 2D program such as Photoshop or Painter, and even a kind of photograph shoot by a camera, so that the object will look a lot more convincing.

Rigging Characters

Once you have designed and build your 3D character you need to add bones to the polygon to make it move. Basic rigging involves building a skeleton and skinning the character. Animators then test movement possibilities. Modeling, rigging, and animation continue until all problems have been resolved. The primary goal of rigging, however, is to make it as direct and easy as possible for the animator to do the job. Software programs also allow actors to be rigged with motion capture sensors, which convert the actor's movement to animation for a predesigned character.

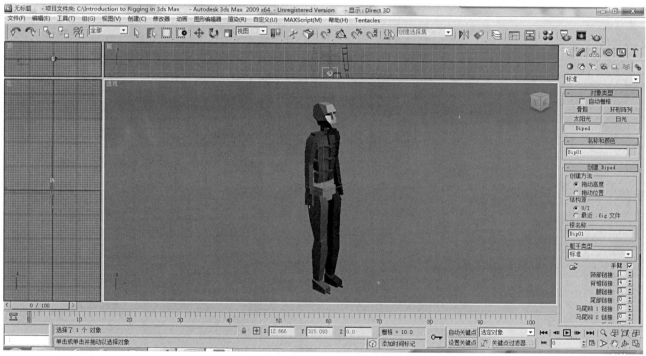

This model was build and animated in 3Ds Max.

Key Frames

Most 3D animation uses a key frame and timeline system, similar to the ones in 2D animation. This means that you set your character or object in an extreme position of the action, move it into the next pose and set it on the timeline, and let the software calculate the inbetweens. After the movement of characters, the limbs, eyes, mouth, clothes, etc. of the figure are moved by the animator on key frames. You could create for yourself a library of facial expressions and use the morpher to change from one expression to another, or you could build a face using 'bones'.

Lighting

Lighting becomes the major focus after animation has been completed in each scene. In 3D software, the default ambient light is dull, flat and even. This is not the light that should be used at the rendering stage. Apart from being used to bring a natural luminance to your scenes, lighting gives form to your objects and scene.

For interior settings, using two or three lights is the ideal. The first light is your key light, it supplies the strongest light. The second light is the fill light, it takes the harshness from shadows. The third light is a backlight, it is a low-key light that helps bring the object out of the background. You should try to work with as few lighting sources as possible. For exteriors settings, you have to deal with the original source of all light, the sun. Most 3D software comes with a preset sunlight.

The best way to get as much realism as you can from your lighting is by experimenting with what your software has to offer, and by observing your environment.

Camera Techniques

At this stage, characters are added to the locations and animation improved. Cinematography elements (camera position, angles, movements, lighting) are added and polished. A basic understanding of cinematography will be a great help when you are shooting your film, even if it amounts to no more than knowing the difference between a pan, a dolly shot and a tracking shot. Being able to move and position the camera is vital to making your animation dynamic and realistic, you should try to copy a film camera sense by using different focal length lenses and adjustable depth of field. One of the great advantages of 3D CGI animation is this possibility of trying different ways of shooting before committing to the final render, if really necessary, the chance to 'reshoot' from a different angle.

The secret of good cinematography, just like the secret of good lighting, is that, if you don't notice it, it's successful. You want the viewer to be drawn into the story and on-screen action and not to be overly distracted by the camera's movements.

Rendering

Rendering is probably the least interesting and most technical, and ultimately the most important, part of the 3D animation process. This is where all the polygons, shaders, lights, effects and camera work come together in the final animation.

Rendering a single image or an animation is essentially the same time-consuming process. The computer has to make thousands of complex mathematical calculations to create each single image, and your animation is going to contain hundreds or thousands of these images.

The lighting effects, such as caustics and global illumination, and camera effects, such as depth of field, all put a heavy load on your rendered so you need to decide how vital they are to your scene. Use whatever tricks you can to reduce rendering at the building stage, so that you can concentrate on getting the most from your lighting and other effects. At the professional level, you have to use an external renderer, and the most widely known and used is Mental Ray.

Words and phrases

digitized 数字化的
interior 内部，室内
exterior 外部的，外景
luminance 亮度
harshness 粗糙度
backlight 背光源
low-key 低调的
lenses 镜头
reshoot 补拍
pre-production 前期制作
RAM storage 内存
graphics workstation 图形工作站
processor 处理器
Render Farm 渲染农场
giant computer 巨型计算机
modeling 建模
basic geometric shapes 基本几何形状
wire-frame model 线框模型
shader 着色器，材质
shininess 发亮，自发光
bump 凹凸贴图
glow 辉光
texture map 纹理贴图
polygon 多边形
skin 蒙皮
motion capture sensors 动作捕捉传感器
timeline 时间轴，时间线
morpher 变形器
preset 预设
cinematography 电影艺术
dolly shot 推拉镜头
tracking shot 跟拍镜头
depth of field 景深
caustics 焦散
global illumination 全局光，全局照明
external renderer 外部渲染器

Practice

1. Review and summarize the general production process of 3D animation.
2. How to create character in 3D software?
3. How to control facial expression in 3D animation?

Translate into English

1. 对于三维动画而言，重要的不是电脑技术而是故事本身。

2. 在三维软件里要先创建角色模型，然后将虚拟的骨架绑定到角色模型上，通过控制骨骼来让角色动起来。

3. 实现真实光照效果的最好方法就是用软件能够提供的功能反复尝试，并且要注意观察真实的环境。

Further reading

3D Animation Essentials
Editor: Andy Beane
Publisher: Sybex (2012)

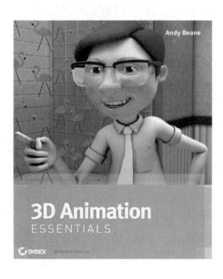

Web links

www.lynda.com

Translation of text

由于电脑的普及，三维动画片越来越多，这让我们很高兴。但是最关键的不是技术而是故事本身。这就是为什么皮克斯的动画片这么受欢迎，不是因为神奇的渲染软件或者逼真的毛皮，而是因为故事和角色本身就很精彩。

三维动画和二维动画的创作方法不同，但是前期和后期制作，比如脚本、故事板、角色设计等都是一样的。本小节将讲解用可购买的软件制作三维动画的基本知识。

设备

现在几乎每个人都可以拥有一台好电脑，但是你要知道三维动画软件要求电脑内存要大、硬盘要大，以便存储制作动画电影所需要的大量文件。现如今，很多强大的工作站取代了家用电脑。图形工作站通常用两核或四核处理器，这样运算能力要强于家用电脑，专门用来做三维渲染。大量的工作站用网络连接在一起（比如渲染农场）就可以充当一个巨型计算机。工作站越贵，渲染的速度越快，因为它们配有技术更先进的硬件。

软件

你要做的动画片的类型是选择动画软件的原因之一。最高端的商业套装软件比如 Maya、3Ds Max 是非常全面并无所不能的软件。现在这两款软件都在 Autodesk 旗下，而且它们之间的差别越来越小。

建模

设计工作要先用二维的方式来完成，通过后才能三维建模。角色在电脑里建模，通常从最基本的几何体开始，然后将各部分细节黏合到一起或者用数字化方式雕塑成一个线框模型。大部分三维软件把界面分成四个摄像机视角，这样当你操作对象的时候就可以清楚地看到发生了什么。

在三维动画里，虽然不需要将动作的每一帧都做出来，但是也需要将片子里出现的所有东西就创建出来。在这一阶段，你需要创建整个场景，不论是室内空间还是外部空间，包括场地、物品、道具和环境等。想要场景更逼真，就需要做更多的创建工作。

材质和纹理

材质和纹理是三维动画的一个重要组成部分，它们可以让物体的表面呈现出逼真的效果。

材质控制物体表面的整体外观，大部分材质分为七个不同的元素：颜色、高光、发光、凹凸、反射、透明度、折射和辉光。这些可以单独或混合在一起来创造理想的效果。每个软件都有自己处理此功能的方法，但是和建模一样，基本原理是相同的。

根据不同的效果，你还需要使用纹理贴图，它们是一种应用在物体表面的贴图。这种贴图通常使用二维软件来制作，比如 Photoshop 和 Painter，甚至还可以用相机拍摄的照片，这样做出来的物体看起来更有说服力。

角色绑定

完成三维角色设计、建模之后需要给多边形模型加入骨骼使其动起来。最基本的骨骼绑定包括创建一套骨骼并且蒙皮，之后动画师做动作测试，并反复调整模型、绑定和动画，直到没有任何问题为止。绑定的主要目标就是让动画师操作起来尽可能的直接、容易。三维软件也可以通过运动捕捉设备来捕捉演员的动作，并将其转化成角色的动作。

关键帧

大部分三维动画都使用关键帧和时间线的方法，类似于二维动画的一拍一。这就意味着你要给角色或者物品的动作设置关键的位置，然后移动到下一个姿势并在时间线上打上关键帧，让软件自动计算过渡的中间位置。角色动作完成后，角色的四肢、眼睛、嘴巴、衣服等处的动作也要由动画师来完成。你可以给自己创建一个表情库并用变形器来做表情变换，或者用骨骼来控制面部表情。

灯光

每个场景的动画完成后就要关注灯光设置。在三维软件里，默认的环境光很平没有变化。这不是在渲染阶段要有的灯光。灯光除了能给场景最自然的照明效果，还可以用来表现场景和物体的形态。

对于室内场景，用两盏或三盏灯是最理想的。第一盏灯是主光源，它提供最强的光照。第二个灯是补充光源，用来制造阴影。第三个是背景光，这是一个不太明显的灯光用来将物体从背景中衬托出来。你应该尽可能地用较少的灯光来实现想要的效果。对于室外场景，你必须处理所有光照的原始来源，即太阳光。大部分三维软件都有预设的太阳光。

实现真实光照效果的最好方法就是用软件能够提供的功能反复尝试，并且要注意观察真实的环境。

摄像机技术

在这一阶段，要把角色放到场景里并进一步改进动画。加入并美化摄影元素（摄像机位置、角度、移动、光影）。在摄制影片时要对摄影艺术的基础有所了解，即使你只知道摇镜头、移镜头和跟踪镜头的差别也会给你很大的帮助。适当地移动和放置摄像机对动画的动感和逼真是非常关键的，你应该尝试用可调整焦距和景深的摄像机来模仿电影拍摄的感觉。电脑动画最大的优势是在最终渲染之前可以尝试不同的拍摄方法，如果有必要，则需要从不同的角度重新拍摄。

好的摄影的秘密和灯光设置一样，如果自然到你没有注意到它，那就成功了。你应该将观众吸引到故事中或者屏幕动作上，而不是因为摄像机的移动而分心。

渲染

渲染过程虽然很无聊，但却是三维动画制作过程中最重要的环节。在这个阶段所有的多边形、材质、灯光、特效和摄像机移动将被整合在一起渲染成最终的动画片。

不论是渲染一张静帧图片还是一部动画，从本质上来说都是同样耗费时间的过程。电脑要经过数以千计复杂的数学运算才能生成一张图片，而动画片又是由数以千计这样的图片组成的。

像焦散和全局光这样的灯光特效，以及像景深这样的摄像机特效，给渲染加重了负担，所以你必须判断这些特效对你的场景有多重要。在建模阶段就可以使用各种技巧来降低渲染难度，这样你就可以专注于灯光照明和其他效果。在专业级别，你需要外挂的渲染器插件来做最终渲染，最有名的渲染器插件是 Mental Ray。

2.5 The Process of Stop-Motion Animation
定格动画的创作流程

Text

Some animators prefer to work with puppets, using clay, a plastic material, or foam. These projects are more like live-action films. Characters must be made, sets built, and lighting rigged. Some people work with paper cutouts, sand, or pinscreens. For stop-motion animation, a digital video or camera is placed on a tripod so the action can be filmed frame by frame, moving characters, objects, and camera after almost every frame.

1. Getting Equipped

If you have chosen to work in stop-motion animation, the equipment you will need is a camera, a tripod, and some lights.

（1）Camera

The important thing is to buy the best you can afford, whether it is new or secondhand. Choose a camera or a video camera, and these also come with a removable memory card. As a beginner, try out animation with an inexpensive animation software and a DV camera or webcam, this will get you started.

（2）Tripods

A sturdy tripod is essential. And no matter in which format you shoot, your tripod has got to be rock steady. When making your first films, to concentrate on the animation rather than trying to create flashy camera moves, a locked-off friction head is the best choice. If you have to do a camera move, a Manfrotto geared head gives you more control over your camera movements.

（3）Lighting

Daylight condition is not an option with animation, it is important for the lighting to remain consistent throughout the shooting period. So you need to create an artificially lit set.

The simplest form of low-cost lighting would be with articulated desk lamp, so long as they can be locked off tightly and don't move during your shot. Sheets of white polystyrene board or white card are useful as "fill". Placed opposite the lights, they are used to take away the black shadows created by strong lighting.

2. Software

We also need frame capture software. It allows you to capture your animation with a camera, and feed images into a computer. This way, you can see how your animation is progressing frame by frame. You should be able to overlay your live image over your stored image, and see exactly how far to move limbs, drapery and hairs. You can go backwards and forwards frame by frame, or set up a loop, to show the animation in real time.

3. Script

When writing a script, the main thing to remember is that you must entertain. And that doesn't mean you have to be funny. Entertaining people is making sure that they have really engaged with your idea, and they get some emotion from it. If your ideas are too obscure you will diminish your audience. It's better to give your characters a history. This will help your animation later, and help them develop as real characters for your audience.

4. Planning Your Shots

When you have a script you need to really start putting your characters in context. In order to storyboard your film, you have to first make some visualizations: drawings of what the scenes will look like; the world your characters inhabit.

5. Storyboard

Storyboarding is the most important planning stage of filmmaking. As you realize each image, you need to be thinking about the composition of each shot, the camera angles and the progression of one shot to the next.

Everyone involved in your film can get information from your storyboard. The set designer can see the scale and size of the set, and the cameraperson will begin to resource their kit (lenses, tracks, camera height) from the information on your storyboard.

6. Animatics

Once you have the whole storyboard done you can edit the storyboard itself, moving pictures around, adding or taking away scenes. This helps you to work out your film before you start spending money on sets, voice recording and model making. Stop-motion animation, it is planned down to the smallest detail before you start a shot.

An experienced editor brings a fresh eye to your production and can see what works and what doesn't. They will edit and make more detailed decisions about the film. It may be that you've missed a vital shot, or maybe some scenes are actually superfluous in the telling of the story.

7. Character Design

Once the animatic has been approved, it's time to design the characters. Don't be constrained in your ideas by technical considerations, but when you are designing your characters, think about how they will relate to each other in size and style. If you are designing and building your own puppet, you will need to draw it to scale on graph paper, and think about materials and structure.

You will want to take the following into account when designing your puppet/model:

(1) What of their size, proportion and weight? The proportion for puppets of average size seems to be about 20~25 cm. If you need to go to close-up it would be worth making something on a bigger scale so that textures look good on camera.

(2) How much does it need to bend? This will dictate how strong your armature needs to be, what to make it out of and where the weak points may be.

(3) How subtle will the movements need to be?

(4) How robust does it need to be? Do you intend to use it for a feature? A short film? Will you need to make copies?

(5) How will it stay fixed to the floor for each shot?

(6) Do all parts need to move? Maybe certain parts of the body could be made with hard materials. Take this into account when preparing moulds.

8. Making Your Own Puppet

The puppet described below has been designed with low cost, its flexibility is demonstrated, and it is more robust and easier to handle. It is made with a variety of materials, each dependent on a different model-making process. The puppet contains a wire armature, covered with foam body and clothing, and includes silicone, Milliput and other modelling staples.

Model in standard pose.

(1) Armature

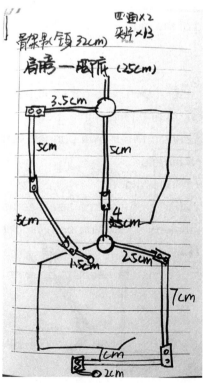

Drawing of the armature.

First of all, get three lengths of 1.5 mm wire twisted together to make the limbs and the spine, and a single strand of 1 mm wire for the wrists, looped round a washer for the palm, and twisted. Washers are epoxy glued to the wrist wire to form the palm of the hand.

Glue on sections of square brass sleeving K&S of sizes that will slot into each other for arms and hands, and head and neck. K&S is square brass tubing that you can buy in any model shop. An M3 nut is soldered onto the larger piece of K&S at the wrist, neck and ankles. This in turn holds the wire in place. The strands of wire are then epoxy glued into the relevant pieces of K&S to form the armature. Steel plate cut with a junior hacksaw is soldered to the three pieces of K&S on the chest piece using silver solder.

Leave enough space for the wire to bend so that the strain is not always on exactly the same spot. Too small a gap between them will make it easier to break.

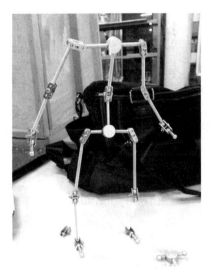

Finishing the wire armature.

(2) Head

It is useful to be able to remove the head and hands for sculpting, leaving the puppet in position. It also means less wear and tear on the puppet. If you are using a clay head, always model the head with a lightweight core to the rear, to allow for eye sockets and a recessed mouth.

(3) Hair

The puppet's hair has been made with Milliput, with a Plasticine-covered wire attached for the ponytail.

(4) Eyes

The easiest way to make eyes is using white glass beads, using the hole as a pupil that can be manipulated with a toothpick. You can also buy eyes from specialist manufacturer or cast them yourself out of resin.

(5) Hands

Hands can be just made with Plasticine on its own or, if you want to make it stronger, over an armature of fine aluminium twisted wire fingers stuck in a resin palm.

(6) Feet

Feet can be made with flat metal plates or aluminium blocks. It is best to make feet with two plates, as a convincing walk is very hard to achieve with a solid, flat foot.

(7) Body

To cover the body, we could choose snip foam. Other choices could be to cover her fully in Plasticine or with foam latex. Snip foam is cheap, light and easily shaped. It is snipped into shape and glued on with a contact adhesive.

(8) Cloth

Clothing it involves a hunt for fine-textured fabric that will nevertheless be robust with constant handling. Once covered with fabric, you have an individual, highly expressive-looking puppet.

9. Sets and Props

In the early planning stages the director and DOP (director of photography) would go through the set design, working out the camera angles, depth of field and so on, with the set designers. Then a mock-up of the sets would be made to scale.

Computer-aided design is a useful way of trying out a set first. A virtual set can be built in the computer, allowing the camera to fly through, check angles and lenses before committing the budget. Again, lighting set-ups can be tried and tested this way.

The model-making department is in charge of all the landscapes, buildings props, furniture, etc. as many of the same skills and materials are used. It is dependent on inventiveness and attention to detail. Model makers all have different feelings as to which materials they use for different purposes.

10. The Production Process

The process of stop-motion animation is much like a live performance and each shot is unique, if you have to do it twice it may be better or worse but it can never be the same.

In the process of stop-motion animation, you have to control all the elements, the weather, the timing and the lighting conditions. Once you have your script, storyboard, sets built, models made, sound breakdown and animation instructions on your X-sheet, you are ready to shoot. You will need to have your camera positions planned, and then set the lighting for your first scene.

(1) Lighting

In a traditional lighting set-up you would have a key light, a fill light and a back light. Multiple shadows can create confusion, so try to keep one main light source or direction, and keep the other lighting soft, by reflecting or diffusing it.

(2) Depth of Field

Your depth of field means the area of your shot that is in focus. In animation, because you are working on a small scale, very much closer to the action, your depth of field is much more critical. Closing down your lens aperture or using a wide-angle lens can increase the depth of field.

(3) Setting up the Camera

All your shooting angles and camera moves should be planned in the storyboard, which will save you time setting up. Check when you set it up that the position you have is correct for the entire shot. Once the camera is in position with the correct zoom, focus and aperture, everything should be locked off: the tripod taped or even glued to the ground.

(4) Blocking out Your Shots

Make time on your shoot to block out your shots first, it is another step in the process that helps you be sure of your moves. You can refer to the frames of your animatic, and place your puppet in its key positions on the set and hold it there for the amount of frames you have doped for those moves. This way you are able to check the lighting, the framing and composition before you embark on the final shoot.

(5) Shooting with DV or Digital Still Camera

Make sure your camera is fixed firmly in position and everything is set as you need so that you no longer have to touch any of the controls, your lens cap is off and you have white balanced. As you shoot each sequence lay it into your animatic, replacing the rough scenes with the finished article.

11. Post-production

(1) Edit

If you have been working with a small budget, you will have edited the film as much as possible in advance with the storyboard, and only need to edit the film in terms of a few frames cut out here and there. However, if you have had a bit more spare time and money you will have given the shots a little overlap at the start and finish, to allow a bit more leeway at the edit stage. This will help achieve smoother edits when cutting on a move.

(2) Sound

When your picture edit is complete, it's time for the soundtrack, this is where sound design really matters. Music, the characters' voices and the layers of sound enhance the mood of the film. You will also need all the atmosphere sounds that make up that scene. The choice of music is very important, the right music can really lift a film.

The sound editors treats the sounds using different recording techniques, and create effects such as footsteps, wings flapping and knuckles cracking, sounds that need to be matched in time to an action on the film.

(3) Titles and Credits

Finally, you need to put on the titles and credits. Be aware in what environment your film may be screened. Don't make the type too small either for big screen or for TV. If you want rolling credits, work on your instinct for timing, neither too fast nor too slow.

(4) Exporting Your Final Film

You may need to convert your film into different formats for distribution. For sending files via the internet or uploading to YouTube, you'll need to make it into a viewable file: WMV, AVI, MOV or MPG. Festivals will require a viewing copy, this could be a DVD, VHS or Mini DV. If your film is selected, they will ask for a screening copy, which could be a Mini DV, a Beta or HDV.

Words and phrases

    foam 泡沫，泡沫体，泡沫塑料
    pinscreen 针幕动画
    tripod 三脚架
    overlay 叠加，覆盖
    proportion 比例
    armature 支架，骨架
    mould 模具，模子
    silicone 硅胶
    spine 脊柱，脊椎
    washer 垫圈
    epoxy 环氧树脂
    glue 粘合，胶
    slot 开槽于……
    soldered 焊接的
    hacksaw 钢锯
    strain 张力，拉紧
    ponytail 马尾辫
    bead 珠子
    pupil 瞳孔
    aluminium 铝
    latex 乳胶，乳液
    adhesive 胶粘剂
    fine-textured 细纹的
    mock-up 伪装工事，实物模型
    diffuse 漫射，散布，传播
    aperture 光圈
    dope 混杂
    knuckle 指关节
    kit 工具箱，成套工具，装备
    removable memory card 可移动记忆卡
    artificially lit set 人为照明设置
    set designer 布景设计师
    cameraperson （尤指电影或电视）摄影师
    square brass sleeving 方形黄铜管
    computer-aided design 电脑辅助设计

Practice

1. Review and summarize the general production process of stop-motion animation.
2. How to make a complete puppet?

Translate into English

1. 好的动画要能让观众一直沉浸在影片的情节当中，然后产生情感的共鸣。
2. 定格动画不适合在自然光照条件下制作，所以要创造一个可以控制的照明环境，并在整个拍摄期间保持一致。
3. 定格动画可以用各种各样的材料来制作，包括沙土、黏土、剪纸等。

Further reading

Stop Motion: Craft Skills for Model Animation
Editor: Susannah Shaw
Publisher: Focal Press (2008)

The Advanced Art of Stop-Motion Animation
Editor: Ken A. Priebe
Publisher: Course Technology PTR (2010)

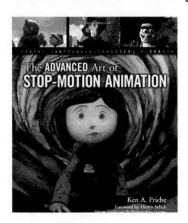

Web links

www.stopmotionanimation.com

Translation of text

有些动画家喜欢用人偶、黏土、塑性材料或者泡沫来做动画。这些动画很像真人电影。要做出角色，建出场景，设定好灯光。有的人还用剪纸、沙土或者针幕来做动画。拍摄定格动画，要将数码摄像机或者数码相机安置在三脚架上，这样动作就可以被逐帧拍摄，每一帧后接着移动角色、物体和数码相机。

1. 所需设备

如果你选择制作定格动画，所需要的主要设备是相机、三脚架和灯光。

（1）相机

对于设备最重要的是在你能承受的范围内选择最好的，不论是新的还是二手的。你可以选择用摄像机或者相机来拍摄，它们都带有记忆卡。作为一个初学者你完全可以用便宜的动画软件和家用 DV 摄像机甚至网络摄像头来制作动画，这会让你学到很多。

（2）三脚架

有一个稳固的三脚架是至关重要的。不管你用何种方式拍摄，你的三脚架都必须像磐石一样稳固。在制作你的第一部动画时，应该将注意力放在动画本身而不是试图创建超酷的相机移动，简易的阻尼式云台系统是最好的选择。如果你需要进行移动拍摄，曼富图齿轮式云台可以给你更多的自由度来控制你的摄像机。

（3）灯光照明

自然日光的光照条件是不适合动画的。在整个拍摄期间保持一致的照明是非常重要的。所以，你要去创造一个可以控制的照明环境。

最简单的低成本照明可以由工作台灯实现。只要它们能被牢牢地固定住而不至于在你拍摄时发生移动就可以了。白色的聚苯板或者白卡纸是很有用的补光工具。它们可以作为反向光源，以削弱因强光照射而产生的黑影。

2. 动画软件

我们还需要帧捕捉软件。它可以让你用相机拍摄动画片段并传输到电脑里。这样，你可以清楚地看到你的动画是如何一帧一帧地处理的。你可以将实时画面覆叠在已经存储的画面上，然后对肢体、服装和头发进行精确的操作。你可以跳回前一帧，也可以跳到后一帧，或者设定一段循环回放，实时地看到动画片段。

3. 脚本

当你写脚本的时候，要记住最重要的是必须有娱乐性，但这并不意味着你需要做得很搞笑。对观众而言，有娱乐性的片子可以让他们一直沉浸在影片中，然后产生情感共鸣。如果你想表达的东西太模糊不清，那么观众很可能就被弄糊涂进而失去兴趣。最好给你的角色设定一个个人小传。这在后面的动画制作中会起到很大的作用，能帮助你让角色发展出真正的个性。

4. 设计镜头

脚本完成后，需要把角色放在情节当中。为了把剧本变成分镜头脚本，需要先将你的构想视觉化：画出想要的场景感觉，画出角色生活的环境。

5. 故事板

故事板的绘制是整个动画制作过程当中最重要的一个环节。在设定了每个静止的影像之后，你需要考虑每个镜头的构成、摄像机的角度和如何进行镜头间的切换。

制作团队中的每一个人都可以从你的故事板当中获得信息。场景设计师可以由此决定场景的规模和大小，摄影师则可以开始组合他的装备（镜头、轨道和高度）。

6. 动态分镜

当整个故事板完成之后，你就可以开始剪辑故事板了。将这些图片变换顺序，看看需要加上或者删去什么场景。这个过程可以帮助你在设备、声音录制和建模上投入资金之前了解整个影片的效果。定格动画需要在开始拍摄之前预定好每一个小细节。

经验丰富的剪辑师会判断出什么是可以实现的而什么不能实现。他们会剪辑并且作出一些更具体的决定。这是因为也许一些镜头在你讲述故事的过程当中并不需要，而有的重要的镜头却被漏掉了。

7. 角色设计

动态分镜通过后，就可以开始做角色设计了。不要因为技术顾虑而束缚你的想法，但是当你设计角色的时候，要考虑一下他们在尺寸比例和风格上的关系。当你设计和制作人偶时，有必要将它以同等比例画在方格纸上，并要考虑材料和结构。

当你在设计你的人偶或模型时你得考虑以下问题：

（1）人偶的具体尺寸、比例和重量。人偶的平均大小为20~25厘米。如果你需要拍摄特写，就要做一个放大版的人偶，这样纹理会拍摄得很清楚。

（2）需要弯曲多少？这取决于你骨架的强度，由什么材料制成以及最脆弱的部位在哪。

（3）动作需要怎样的敏锐度？

（4）角色需要有多强壮？你打算用于制作一部长动画片？短片？需要多做几个备用么？

（5）每次拍摄时需要如何固定在地面上？

（6）所有部分都需要动么？或许身体的某些部分需要用硬质材料来做。在准备制作模型时把这一点考虑进去。

8. 制作人偶

以下讲述的人偶是低成本的制作，灵活性很好，而且结实更易于操作。它由各种材料组成，每种材料的制作工序都不同。人偶包含一个金属骨架，覆盖了泡沫的躯体和衣服，还包括树脂、复合黏土和用于模型制作的卡钉。

（1）金属骨架

首先，把三股直径为1.5毫米的金属丝拧在一起分别制作上下肢和脊柱，再单独用一根1毫米金属丝制作腕关节，环绕成手掌心垫圈，再缠紧。垫圈则用二合一混合胶粘合成手掌心形状。

可以将几段K&S分别插入手臂和双手、头部和颈部。K&S是一种方形黄铜软管，在任何一家模型店皆可购买。用一个M3螺母在腕关节、颈部和脚踝处焊接到更大的K&S上。相应的，这也使金属丝定形了。再用二合一混合胶将这些金属丝粘到相应的K&S上让骨架定形。用银质焊料来将手工切割的钢板焊接到胸前的三段K&S上。

为金属丝预留足够的弯曲空间，这样拉紧时张力不会总在同一个点上。如果它们之间缝隙太小容易使骨架断裂。

（2）头部

在造型过程中，能在不影响人偶动作的前提下移动头部和手臂是很有用的。这还意味着人偶穿着更少并且被破坏得更少。如果你使用黏土做头部，通常用一个轻材质的内核放在头的后部，这样能为放眼睛的眼窝和安放嘴部的槽提供空间。

（3）头发

人偶的头发由复合黏土制成，用橡皮泥覆盖的金属丝来连接人偶的马尾辫。

（4）眼睛

制作眼睛最简单的方法是用白色玻璃珠，用上面的洞做瞳孔并且可以用牙签来操作。你也可以从专业制造商处购买眼睛或者自己用树脂浇注。

（5）双手

手可以直接用橡皮泥制作，或者要是你想使它更坚固些，可以在一个铝丝骨架上缠好金属手指再插入树脂掌心。

（6）双脚

脚部可以用扁平金属板或铝块制作。最好用两块金属板制作脚部，因为一只固体的、扁平的脚很难做到有力地行走。

（7）身体

我们可以选择可剪裁的泡沫来覆盖人偶的身体。另外还可以用橡皮泥，或者使用泡沫乳胶。可剪裁的泡沫很便宜，而且很轻，也容易造型。剪成所需形状后用万能胶粘起来。

（8）衣服

给人偶缝制衣服需要用好面料，这样即使反复操作也很结实。只要加上衣服，你就有一个独立的、能传情达意的漂亮人偶了。

9. 场景和道具

在计划的早期阶段，总导演和摄影指导将会过一遍场景设计，和场景设计师一起研究拍摄角度和景深等。然后场景的缩小版模型将被制作出来。

计算机辅助设计是一种初步建立场景的有效方式，在制作场景之前，可以先在计算机上建立一个虚拟场景，在花费预算之前，让软件中的镜头穿过场景来检测角度和镜头位置。

模型制造部门负责景观、建筑道具、家具的制作，会用到很多相似的技巧和材料，这取决于工作人员对细节的专注和创造力。模型师根据自己的感觉和经验决定使用不同的材料去表达不同的目的。

10. 拍摄过程

定格动画的拍摄过程很像是一种现场演出，每个镜头都是独一无二的。如果你不得不重来一遍，效果好坏都有可能，但永不可能再获得相同的效果。

在定格动画的拍摄过程中，你必须控制所有的元素，天气、时间以及照明。一旦你把剧本、故事板、布景准备好，模型做好，把声音剪切好以及把动画制作注明在摄影表上，就准备好开拍了。你需要设计好摄像机位置，然后为第一个场景设置灯光。

（1）灯光照明

按传统灯光设置来说，你得有一个主光、一个补光以及一个背景光。阴影过多会产生混乱，因此尽量采用一个主要光源或光照方向，同时以折射或散射的方式让其他灯光保持柔和。

（2）景深

景深意味着清晰对焦区域的大小。对于动画制作而言，因为拍摄场景比例很小，拍摄距离要近得多，因此景深因素便更为关键。缩小光圈或者使用广角镜头都能有效增加景深。

（3）架设摄像机

所有的拍摄角度和摄像机运动都应该提前在故事板上规划好，这样会节省你的架设时间。架设好后应检查位置是否适合整个镜头。一旦摄像机位置确定，缩放、焦距以及光圈都已设置好，就要把这一切都固定下来，三脚架应用胶带甚至粘胶固定在地上。

（4）镜头彩排

从拍摄安排中分出一些时间来进行镜头彩排，这样可以进一步帮助你确保动作的正确性。你可以参考动态分镜里的每一帧，将人偶依次置于布景内的各个关键位置，然后针对不同动作所规划的所有帧进行彩排。通过这个办法，你就能在最终开拍之前对灯光、帧的设计以及合成进行检查。

（5）用DV或者数码相机拍摄

确定摄像机已固定好，而且一切都已根据需要设置正确，这样就不再需要触碰任何控制部件，取下镜头盖，调好白平衡。每完成一段拍摄，便可放入动态分镜里，用这些已完成的镜头替换草稿。

11. 后期制作

（1）画面剪辑

如果你一直是在缺少经费的情况下制作，你可以提前在故事板策划阶段就开始尽可能地对影片进行剪辑，也可以仅对个别帧进行剪辑。然而，如果你的时间和金钱都比较充裕的话，那不妨在镜头开始与结尾时多拍出一些重叠部分，这样在剪辑阶段就会有更多余地。这也有助于在剪辑一段动作时获得更平滑的效果。

（2）音效

完成画面剪辑后，就是处理音轨的时间了，这正是音效设计的关键之处。音乐、角色的声音以及声音的层次都会增强影片的情绪。你还需要有完整的背景音效来营造出场景的气氛。如果音乐正好合适，那再好不过，但是音乐的选取极为重要，好的音乐能提升一部影片的层次。

音效师用不同的录制技巧来处理声音，而且要制作出多种音效，如脚步声、拍动翅膀的声音以及关节响声，声音需要与影片的动作对位。

（3）字幕与致谢名单

最后，你需要加上字幕和致谢名单。需要注意影片会在什么环境下播放。不管是在大屏幕上还是电视上播放，都不要把字体做得太小。如果你决定使用滚动致谢名单，可凭直觉掌控时间，只是不要太快或者太慢。

（4）导出最终影片

根据发行的要求，你可能有必要将影片转换为不同的格式。如果是要通过互联网传送影片，或是要将其上传至YouTube，你需要将其做成以下格式的视频文件：WMV、AVI、MOV或者MPG。电影节会需要你寄一份评审拷贝，可以是DVD、VHS或Mini DV的形式。如果你的影片入选，主办方还会要求你提供放映拷贝，可以是Mini DV、Beta或HDV的形式。

Unit 3　Responsibilities of Animation Makers
第3单元　动画制作者的职责

3.1　Animated Movie Director
动画电影导演

Text

　　Just like a live-action director, the Animated Movie Director is the main creative force on the project. He supervises just about everything, including story, dialogue recording, modeling, animation, post-production, and tinkers with every aspect of the production process. There may be more than one director. Many feature-length animations split directorial duties between two people. Generally, one director will deal with the acting portion of the movie, while the other deals with the artistic and technical aspects of the movie. Many animated television series will have a dialogue director and a separate animation director.

　　The first step of an animated movie is the scriptwriter. Some production studios require a script before production begins. Others, like Pixar, come up with a concept first, then let the plot and characters evolve alongside the visuals. As the first visualization of the script, the storyboard must be approved by the producer and director. Then, artists present the director with rough sketches of the characters, settings, and props. In computer animation, they'll translate these 2D images into 3D renderings early on, but these models can be manipulated and tweaked endlessly. Then, with the director's guidance, artists will map out the storyboard, drawing detailed pictures for every shot in the project.

　　The director also has a hand in recording the characters' voices. Normally, actors record dialogue before the real animating begins, that way, animators know when and how to move the characters' mouths. This means that the context of the scene isn't always obvious—and it's the director's job to fill in the details.

　　Once the dialogue is recorded, the soundtrack is cut together with the entire storyboard to produce animatic. Different characters are assigned to different animators according to skills and abilities. Some are better at drawing realistic characters, others at cartoony characters. Some specialize in faces and emotion, while others excel at movements and slapstick gestures. The director also chooses background animators, they are the digital equivalent of set designers.

　　Directors usually work with animators. They must have a good understanding of animation principles, mechanics, movements, style and continuity. First they sit down with the storyboards and describe exactly what they want. Sometimes they'll even act it out. The animator then takes a first crack at animating the segment frame by frame and shows the result to the director, who makes tweaks. Directors bring their own personal style to this process. As each scene is completed, it gets slotted into the animatic slide show. This way, the director can see the film coming together scene by scene.

Once the visuals are near-final, the meaning major changes are no longer permitted. At that point, the director brings in a composer and a sound-effects designer to record music and background noises. The sound mixer then overlays these elements onto the prerecorded dialogue. Again, the director's job is to preserve the overall vision, to make sure every element fits together.

No specific education is required to become an Animated Movie Director, but directors usually complete a 2 or 4 year degree in filmmaking, and Animated Movie Directors are almost always experienced animators. Modern animation techniques rely heavily upon CGI, and it's important to be familiar with current technologies. Training in the fundamentals of art history and visual art is equally important. Associate or bachelor degrees in art, computer animation or filmmaking are good places to start your career as an Animated Movie Director.

Words and phrases

Animated Movie Director　动画电影导演
supervise　监督，管理，指导
feature-length animation　长片动画
animated television series　动画电视连续剧
animation director　动画导演
scriptwriter　编剧
concept　概念
plot　情节
tweak　调整
slapstick　粗俗的滑稽剧，闹剧
equivalent　相等的
mechanics　力学
composer　作曲家
sound-effects designer　音响效果设计师
sound mixer　混音师
filmmaking　电影摄制，电影制作，影视制作
fundamental　基本原理，基本原则
bachelor degree　学士学位

Practice

1. What are the main responsibilities of Animated Movie Director?
2. Talk about the difference between Animated Movie Director and animation director.

Translate into English

1. 导演会将自己的个人风格带入到整个片子里。
2. 动画电影导演是整个项目的核心人物,他负责监督和指导片子的各个方面。

Further reading

Directing for Animation: Everything You Didn't Learn in Art School
Editor: Tony Bancroft
Publisher: Focal Press (2013)

Web links

www.pixar.com

Translation of text

像真人电影导演一样,动画电影导演是整个片子的主要创作力量。他监督所有工作,包括故事编写、对白录制、建模、动画、后期制作以及对整个片子的各个方面做出修改。有的时候不只有一位导演。许多动画长片将导演的工作分给两个人。一般来说,其中一位导演负责片子的制作部分,另一位则负责艺术效果和技术部分。许多电视动画系列片还会有对白导演和单独的动画导演。

动画电影的第一步是剧本。很多动画工作室在项目开始之前会先有一个脚本。其他的,像皮克斯会先从概念设计开始,然后将情节和角色的发展可视化。作为脚本的第一个可视化版本,故事板必须由制片人和导演通过。然后,工作人员在导演的带领下绘制角色、场景和道具的草稿。在电脑动画里,在早期他们会将二维图像转化成三维效果图,但是这些模型会被没完没了地进行操作和调整。接着在导演的指导下,工作人员绘制故事板,画出每个镜头的详细图稿。

导演还要负责角色声音的录制。通常,在真正动画开始之前要录制演员的对白,这样动画师就知道角色的嘴什么时候会动。这说明场景的上下文不是一直都很明确,这就需要导演将细节补充好。

一旦对话录制好了,便可将音轨与故事板剪辑在一起从而做成动态分镜。根据动画师的技能他们会分到不同的角色。有些擅长画写实风格的角色,有些则擅长画卡通风格。有些专门画面部和情感表现,而有些则擅长画动作和搞笑的姿势。导演还会挑选合适的背景画师,他们是用电脑绘制场景的设计师。

导演经常和动画师一起工作。他们必须了解动画原理、力学、运动、画面风格和连续性。首先他们一起研究故事板并准确地描述他们想要的东西。有时候他们甚至还会自己表演出来。然后动画师将动画的一个片段的第一个版本逐帧画出来，导演看后要做出修改调整。导演将自己的个人风格带入到整个片子里。当每一个镜头完成后，替换到动态分镜里。这样导演就可以看到整部片子的效果。

当片子接近最终完成的时候，这就意味着不会再做较大的改动。这时，导演会请合成师和音响设计师来录制音乐和环境音。混音器将所有的元素叠加到预先录制的对白上。同样，导演的工作是要保持整体的视觉效果，以确保所有的元素很好地融合在一起。

想成为动画电影导演不需要什么特殊的学历，但是导演通常要在电影制作专业得到一个2或4年制的学位，而且动画电影导演几乎都是很有经验的动画师。现代动画严重依赖电脑技术，熟悉目前最新的技术对动画导演来说很重要。艺术史和视觉艺术的基础知识学习也同样重要。在艺术专业、电脑动画或者电影制作专业得到学士学位或者2年制的副学士学位是开始你动画电影导演职业生涯的好地方。

3.2 Animation Scriptwriters
动画编剧

Text

Writing an animation script is somewhat like directing a film. Scriptwriters are responsible for researching the story, developing the narrative, writing the script in the required format. Scriptwriters have great influence over the creative direction and emotional impact of the script and, arguably, of the finished film. They are almost always freelancers who either pitch original ideas to Producers, or who are commissioned by a Producer to create a script from a concept, true story or literary work, such as a novel, poem, play, comic book or short story. Scriptwriting is emotionally and intellectually demanding, and requires an in-depth understanding of visual storytelling and of the different ways that films affect audiences.

Scriptwriters provide a blueprint onto which the Producer, Director, Production Designer, Composer and Editor, cast and crew can graft their creative efforts. The script must not only feature fascinating characters, an exciting plot, and a great premise for a marketable film, but it must also conform to the logical principles of dramatic construction, as well as to industry expectations regarding format and style. Scriptwriters must produce highly creative writing, to strict deadlines, and they need to work constructively with other members of the script development team to create a product that is likely to be financed and made.

Scriptwriters need to write visually, using sound and dialogue to support the action in order to create a credible and internally consistent story world. They need to understand how a screen work manipulates and entertains its audience, and must be able to structure their work within a specific tone and genre to satisfy and transcend audience expectations.

Writing for animation also involves a lot of other people and their input, ands scriptwriters have to be quite robust, able to take criticism and judge how best to use it when re-writing their work. Dealing with rejection is an integral part of the scriptwriters' craft. They usually have to write many drafts of a script, as well as outlines, treatments and other documents to attract potential investors. Getting an idea onto the screen can be a very long process, requiring determination and stamina.

There are no specific qualifications for a scriptwriter. However, writers with proven storytelling experience in another field, such as theatre dramatists, novelists and journalists.

Words and phrases

Scriptwriter 编剧
narrative 叙事的，叙述
freelancer 自由职业者
commission 委托，授权
literary 文学的，书面的
novel 小说
poem 诗歌
intellectually 理性的，理智地
cast 演职人员
crew 团队，全体人员
graft 脚踏实地地埋头苦干
internally 在内部
genre 类型，流派
rejection 退稿，拒绝，排斥
investor 投资人
stamina 毅力，耐力
qualification 资格证书，职位要求

Practice

1. What are the main responsibilities of Scriptwriter?
2. How to become a Scriptwriter?

Translate into English

1. 编剧可以受制片人的委托将真实的故事或者文学作品如小说、诗歌、戏剧、漫画书或短篇故事改编成动画剧本。
2. 把一个故事搬到屏幕上是一个非常漫长的过程，作为编剧需要具有超然的毅力。

Further reading

How to Make Money Scriptwriting
Editor: Julian Friedmann
Publisher: Intellect Books (2000)

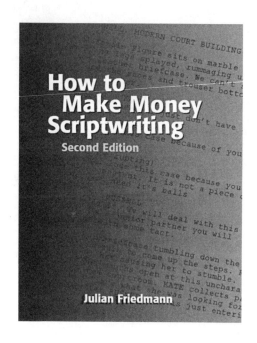

Web links

www.thescreenplaywriters.com

Translation of text

编写动画剧本有点像导演电影。动画编剧负责研究故事、发展情节叙事,按照要求的格式编写脚本。编剧对剧本以及整个片子的创作方向和情感表现有很大的影响力。他们几乎都是自由职业者,既可以把原创的想法推销给制片人,也可以受制片人的委托将一个概念想法、真实的故事或者文学作品如小说、诗歌、戏剧、漫画书或短篇故事改编成动画剧本。编写剧本有情感上和理性上的要求,并且要求对视觉叙事和不同方式对观众的影响有深入的了解。

编剧要向制片人、导演、美术指导、作曲家、剪辑师提供一个蓝图,这样团队工作人员可以发挥他们的创造力努力工作。脚本不仅要有充满魅力的角色、扣人心弦的情节、适销对路的前提,还要符合戏剧建设的逻辑原则,以及业界要求的格式和风格。编剧的写作必须有高度创造性,严责遵守时间期限,同时要有团队精神从而能够与编剧部门的其他成员一起合作,创作出能被投资并完成的作品。

编剧需要写出画面感,用声音和对话来表现动作以此来创造出一个真实的内在一致的故事环境。他们必须知道一个影视作品是如何运作并娱乐观众的,必须能够创作出一个有特定的基调和风格的作品来满足和超越观众的期望。

给动画写剧本还涉及很多其他人的参与,编剧必须非常有耐心听取批评,并将这些意见在重写剧本时好好利用。处理退稿是编剧工作的一部分。他们通常还有写许多的脚本草稿、故事大纲、解决方案和其他文件来吸引潜在的投资者。把一个故事搬到屏幕上是一个非常漫长的过程,需要有决心和毅力。

要成为动画编剧不需要特别的资历。但是,需要在其他领域有一定的写作经验,比如可以是戏剧作家、小说家或者记者。

3.3 Animators

动画师

Text

Animators breathe life into an image, or give personality to a character, by creating a series of static drawings. In key animation, the animators take the character sheets and start roughing in the actions of the characters. Rough animations allow animators to quickly capture the character's motions without worrying about the details of the character. While working, they place the background layouts under their animation to make sure the characters line up with the proper background elements.

As the animators finish roughing in the main key poses, they start making them look more like the approved character design. They also add in the subtle animation touches such as follow-through, hair movement, subtle emotions, and more.

The lead (also called supervising or key) animator may just draw the key poses showing the motion extremes. The animator will chart where the inbetweens should go. This chart shows how many drawings need to be drawn between the keys and how close each drawing needs to be to the next or previous one.

In addition to charts, the animator may also make notes on the keys drawings as to what needs to be done and what parts of the drawing to pay more attention to. Each drawing also needs to be properly numbered.

When an animator fills out the X-sheet, he also needs to mark the drawings to match. When a character, or characters, are drawn in parts using more than one level of animation, knowing which drawings go on which level is very important. The X-sheet keeps all the art, levels, and timings organized for each scene.

Depending on the project, animators follow a brief from a director, animation director or lead animator, and refer to established designs, models and layouts when creating the movement which will appear on screen. They may work alone, or they may supervise the work of assistants and inbetweeners. They are sometimes responsible for the standard of their team's work and for ensuring that the animation is drawn on model (in style) throughout the process. On other productions, including some feature animation, animators may work only in rough, leaving the clean up department to re-draw and put the animation on model. Animators need to be aware of the production schedule and must deliver their work on brief and on time.

A feel for movement and timing is essential to produce convincing animation, and animators need creative and artistic qualities, along with plenty of patience. For character animation, good drawing and animation experience combined with observational skills and acting talent are all very important. Animators must be able to take direction and work as part of a team. They should also pay attention to detail and have the capacity to communicate clearly with colleagues.

Animators have usually worked previously as inbetweeners or assistants. Certain individuals with particular talent progress very quickly to the role of animator, while others can take much longer to reach that position.

Inbetweeners are responsible for producing neat and accurate drawings between previously completed key poses, in order to complete the illusion of movement and action. This is often an entry-level role in the animation department, and may provide an ideal opportunity to acquire both practical animation skills and a solid foundation for future work.

Although the animators' work may be in rough, inbetweeners are more likely to be asked to produce cleaned up drawings, referring to existing animation and model sheets. They must have enough drawing ability to be able to adapt to the style and technique of different productions, and be aware of their schedule in order to deliver on time.

Words and phrases

key pose　关键姿态
lead animator　动画组长，首席动画师
chart　运动标尺
X-sheet　摄影表
assistant　助手，助理
inbetweener　中间画师
clean up department　清稿部门，清稿组
schedule　时间表，日程安排
capacity　能力，资格
colleague　同事
neat　灵巧的，整洁的，优雅的
accurate　精确的，准确的
entry-level　入门的，初级的，最低阶层的，适合于初学者的

Practice

1. How do animation director, lead animator, assistants, inbetweener and clean up department work together?

2. How to become an eligible animator in the animation department?

Translate into English

1. 动画师负责参照角色标准造型完成关键动作的草稿，他们也会加入一些动画技巧比如跟随动作、头发的动作、微妙的情感等。

2. 对于动画师而言，良好的画功、动画经验、观察力和表演天赋都是非常重要的。

Further reading

Force: Animal Drawing: Animal locomotion and design concepts for animators
Editor: Mike Mattesi
Publisher: Focal Press (2011)

Web links

www.dreamworksanimation.com

Translation of text

动画师的工作是通过绘制一系列的静态图画给图片注入生命，或者给角色赋予个性。做动画的时候，动画师按照角色造型表来开始绘制角色动作的草稿。动画草稿允许动画师快速捕捉角色运动而不用考虑角色的细节。当绘制的时候，他们会把背景构图放在动画的下层来确保角色能够完全和背景元素对齐。

当动画师完成关键动作的草稿后，他们就按照角色标准造型开始修形。他们也会加入一些动画技巧，比如跟随动作、头发的动作、微妙的情感等。

首席动画师会画出关键姿态来表示动作的原画。动画师将在运动标尺中标出什么地方要加入中间画。运动标尺将说明在原画中间要添加多少张中间画以及每张中间画与前后两张的距离。

除了运动标尺，动画师还要在原画上记下哪些图画需要完成以及图画的哪些部分需要额外注意。每幅图也需要做适当的编号。

当动画师在填写摄影表的时候，他还需要标记图画使其与摄影表内容对应。当一个或多个动画角色各部分是分层来做动画的时候，知道哪些图画应该放在哪一层上是非常重要。摄影表将每个镜头的动画、分层和时间都安排好了。

根据不同的动画项目，动画师受导演、动画导演和首席动画师领导，并在绘制动作时要参考已经确定的设计、模型和构图。他们会独立完成工作，或者监督助手和中间画师的工作。这些人有时负责团队工作的标准以及确保动画在绘制过程中都是按照模型来画的。在其他的项目里，包括动画长片，动画师只负责绘制草稿，清稿部门负责重新绘制和修形。动画师需要了解项目进度，以便在规定时间内完成工作。

　　运动感和时间感对于使动画具有说服力是非常重要的，动画师需要有创造力、艺术表现力以及足够的耐心。对于角色动画，良好的画功和动画经验与观察力和表演天赋相结合是非常重要的。动画师要必须能够接受指导并有团队精神。他们也应该注意细节并能够与同事具备良好的沟通能力。

　　动画师通常从中间画师和助手做起。有些特别有天分的人很快就做到动画师了，其他人可能需要很长的时间才能到这个位置。

　　中间画师负责在之前完成的原画中间添加整齐准确的过渡，来完成完整的动作。这通常是动画部门的入门级工作，为习得实用的动画技巧和为今后的工作奠定基础提供了一个很好的机会。

　　因为动画师绘制草稿，所以中间画师往往会被要求参考现有的动画和模型表做清稿工作。他们必须有足够的绘画功底来适应不同动画项目的风格和工艺要求，并且要注意进度从而按时完成工作。

3.4　Art Director
　　艺术总监

Text

　　An art director of animation is an artist who is responsible for conceiving the overall visual styling of a film. He oversees the entire design department and directly supervises the character artists, prop artists, layout artists and color stylists. If there is no designer on the production, the art director is responsible for the look of the film, include the design of the backgrounds, characters, the props, and the color palettes. He must closely work with the animation director to define the animation's graphic style and make sure the entire project tracks to a consistent artistic vision.

　　Usually, the art director of animation work with many people during the concept phase before launching into the pre-production phase. There may also be conceptual illustrators whose drawings inspire the look of the project. The art director is also in charge of the overall visual appearance and how it communicates visually, stimulates moods and psychologically appeals to a target audience. In process of creating a certain product, it is the art director who decides which visual elements to choose, what artistic style to apply and when to use motion.

　　There is no set path to becoming an art director. Most art directors have degrees from art schools, and at least 3 years of successful, progressively responsible experience managing animation teams and projects. In today's job market art directors also need to know various computer programs that allow them to work with everything from photographs to font sizes. Artists who want to become art directors must have leadership and management skills and must be responsible and organized. He is responsible for managing the day-to-day operations for our production department, including a team of animators, storyboard artists and freelance artists. He better has strong fine art training and skills (Illustration, painting, 2D & 3D design), and can manage art workflow and schedules.

Words and phrases

art director　艺术指导，艺术总监
conceive　设想，构思
oversee　监督，监管
phase　阶段
launch　发动，开始
conceptual illustrator　概念插画家
psychologically　心理上地，心理学地
progressively　渐进地，日益增多地
workflow　工作流程

Practice

1. Talk about the main responsibilities of an art director.
2. How to become an excellent art director of animation?

Translate into English

1. 艺术指导负责管理项目制作部门的日常运作，并直接领导角色设计师、道具设计师、构图设计师和颜色设计师。
2. 一名合格的艺术指导必须具备领导才能和管理技巧，而且要负责任并有组织能力。

Further reading

Hayao Miyazaki: Master of Japanese Animation: Films, Themes, Artistry
Editor: Helen McCarthy
Publisher: Stone Bridge Press (1999)

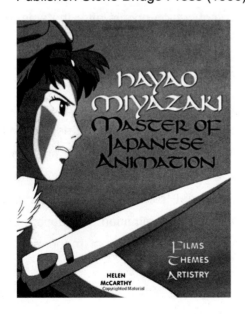

Web links

www.ghibli.jp

Translation of text

动画片的艺术指导负责构思影片的整体视觉风格。他监督整个设计部门并且直接领导角色设计师、道具设计师、构图设计师和颜色设计师。如果项目团队里没有设计师，那么由艺术指导自己完成片子的设计工作，包括角色、道具设计和颜色设定。他必须跟动画导演紧密合作来决定动画的图形风格以及确保整个项目保持一致的艺术效果。

通常，在进入前期制作之前的概念设计阶段，动画片的艺术指导要带领团队工作人员一起工作。会有概念插画师来为片子画概念稿，他们的作品会启发片子的设计灵感。艺术指导也要负责动画的整体视觉效果，以及如何将视觉效果、刺激的情绪气氛和心理诉求传达给目标观众。在项目的制作过程中，是艺术指导来决定视觉元素的选择，适用什么样的艺术风格以及什么时候需要用动作。

成为一个动画片的艺术指导没有固定的方式。大多数艺术指导都有艺术学校的学历，以及至少三年管理动画团队和动画项目的成功经验。在今天的人才市场上艺术指导还需要了解各种电脑软件，可以处理照片和字体等任何东西。想成为艺术指导还必须具备领导才能和管理技巧，而且要负责任并有组织能力。他负责管理项目制作部门的日常运作，包括所有的动画师、故事板艺术家和参与项目的自由职业者。他最好接受过纯艺术培训，有一定的绘画技巧（插图、绘画、二维和三维设计），并且可以管理动画的工作流程和掌握工作进度。

3.5 Compositor and Editor

合成师和剪辑师

Text

Post-production is the final stage of making an animated project, which occurs after the animation has been completed.

Compositor

In post-production of 2D animation, the compositors take all the backgrounds, characters, props, and effects, layers of separate still and motion images together, and seamlessly blend them with the proper camera moves. In 3D animation, they are responsible for constructing the final image by combining layers of previously created material. They need a thorough understanding of the CG process combined with relevant artistic skills. They receive material from various sources which could include rendered computer animation, special effects, graphics, 2D animation, live action, static background plates, etc. Their job is to creatively combine all the elements into the final image, ensuring that the established style of the project is respected and continuity is maintained.

Compositors need to keep up to date with technological developments within their field. They should have extensive knowledge of current compositing software such as Shake and After Effects, and various other programs including Photoshop.

For compositors, probably the most important is the ability to problem analyze and solve. Compositors need the talent to make artistic judgements, the technical skills to take practical decisions. They are also methodical and thorough approach to work, and attention to detail. Often times on a project, image elements are assigned that don't fit together at all and it's the compositor's responsibility to make them seamless and believable when they are composited. Elements might come in a different color space, resolution, or format that compositors presently work in, and they have to make adjustments as needed.

Compositors are likely to have gained a degree in an art-related subject, such as Animation, Design, Illustration, Painting, Photography or Computer Animation. Whether they have received formal training or worked their way up, Compositors need a thorough knowledge of the relevant software currently in use by the industry. Depending on the production, this is most likely to be Shake or After Effects, but could also be Combustion or, possibly Inferno or Flame. As an excellent compositor, both artistic talent and technical skill are needed, however good experiences are likely to be of more value than academic qualifications.

Editor

After the composition, the editor takes all the composited scenes and dialogue and edits them together in the proper sequence, timing the edits such that the story flows with just the right timing.

Unlike live-action production where the editor has lots of footage to choose from when editing, animation has very little, if any, extra footage to edit. In 2D animation, we used every frame of animation we drew in the final edit.

You may find that you need to either lengthen or shorten a cycled sequence to make a scene feel right. Maybe a scene needs a longer hold at the end. Maybe a title card needs to be held longer. These elements may be easily adjusted in editing or compositing. The editor removed and added single frames until it felt just right. The length of a single frame sometimes makes a big difference. The editor also need to rearrange the order of the scenes to have the story make more sense, or to heighten the drama. This happens more than you might think. Working with nonlinear editing systems makes this very easy and fast. Since most 2D animation is digitally painted and composited, we most likely use a digital nonlinear editing program. During editing, editors will compile all of the production elements, title cards, credits, footage, sound effects, music, dialogue, and more. If the project is to be broadcast, editors should also add color bars and tone (a preset audio tone) at the beginning (to allow broadcasters to check color and audio levels) and a countdown leading up to the beginning of the film.

When editors edit the sound in edit program, they can use many levels of overlapping audio for the dialogue, effects, and music, and they need to balance the levels of each so the dialogue is easy to understand and none of the audio is distorted. Editing programs also offer editors many different styles of transitions. The best transitions to use are simple cuts and dissolves. One of the first signs of low-budget animation is bad lip sync. The editors must take great care to match the sync of the new audio to the animation; it will be worth the time.

Words and phrases

compositor　合成师
thorough　彻底的，完全的
relevant　有关的，中肯的，有重大作用的
methodical　有条理的，有方法的
art-related　与艺术相关的，与美术相关的
editor　剪辑师，编辑
footage　影片长度，连续镜头，电影胶片
rearrange　重新排列，重新整理
nonlinear editing system　非线性编辑系统
compile　编译，编辑
transition　转场
dissolve　溶解
low-budget　低成本的，低预算的
lip sync　音画同步，对口型

Practice

1. What do compositor and editor do in process of post-production?
2. What kind of software do compositors and editors usually use?

Translate into English

1. 对一名优秀的合成师而言，最重要的应该是具备分析问题、解决问题的能力。
2. 剪辑师需要重新排列镜头的顺序来使故事有更多的镜头或者增强戏剧效果。

Further reading

The Art of Madagascar: Escape 2 Africa
Editor: Jerry Beck
Publisher: Insight Editions (2008)

Web links

www.blueskystudios.com

Translation of text

后期制作是制作动画项目的最后一步，动画生成后才进入到这一步。

合成师

在二维动画的后期制作里，合成师将所有的背景、角色、道具，和特效、独立分层的静态和动态图像合成到一起，并且用适当的摄像机移动将他们不留痕迹地融合在一起。在三维动画里，他们负责通过合并数层先前制作的素材来生成最终的图像。他们需要深入了解整个电脑动画这一结合相关艺术技能的制作过程。他们集合各种素材，包括电脑渲染的动画、特效、图形、二维动画、真人影片、静帧的背景等。他们的工作就是将所有元素创造性地结合成最终的图像，确保项目的已定风格受到尊重和保持连续性。

合成师需要在自己的领域始终掌握最新的技术。他们应该对最流行的合成软件，像 Shake 和 After Effects，以及包括 Photoshop 在内的其他软件有全面的了解。

对于合成师而言，最重要的应该是分析、解决问题的能力。合成师需要有对艺术美感具备判断力，采取切实可行的技术。他们还需要有条不紊、严谨的工作态度和对细节的关注能力。做项目的时候，通常图像元素的位置不能完全地对位，这就需要合成师来将它们不留痕迹地处理到一起。收集来的素材可能其色彩模式、分辨率或者格式都是不符合合成师要求的，他们必须按照要求对其进行转化调整。

大部分合成师都有与艺术相关的学历，比如动画、设计、插图、绘画、摄影或者电脑动画。不管他们是否接受过正规的培训，合成师都要对目前行业使用的软件有深入的了解。根据动画项目的需要，最常用软件是 Shake 或者 After Effects，但 Combustion 或者 Inferno 和 Flame 也比较常见。作为一名优秀的合成师，需要艺术才华和技术两者兼备，然而好的工作经验比学历更有价值。

剪辑师

合成完成后，剪辑师将所有合成好的镜头、对白和字幕按照适当的顺序排列好，给字幕设定时间，这样整个故事就会按照正确的时间播放。

真人电影的剪辑师在剪辑的时候有很多素材可供其选择使用，动画则不同，几乎没有多余的镜头可供剪辑。在二维动画里，在最终剪辑的时候我们会用到每一帧动画。

你会发现你需要加长或缩短一个循环序列来使一个镜头感觉舒服一些。或者一个镜头的结尾时间需要长一点。或许片名的持续时间要加长。这些元素可以很容易在剪辑或合成阶段调整。剪辑师可以移走或者加入帧来调整直到感觉可以了。一帧的区别有时候会出现不同的效果。剪辑师还需要重新排列镜头的顺序来使故事有更多的镜头或者增强戏剧效果。这种情况经常发生。用非线性编辑软件来操作可以使剪辑又快又容易。由于二维动画现在都是电脑绘制和合成的，因此我们就用电脑非线性编辑软件。在剪辑过程中，剪辑师将收集所有的项目素材、片头标题、演职员名单、镜头、音响效果、音乐、对白及其他。如果片子需要公开播放，剪辑师应该还要在片子的开始之前加入颜色条和音调（预设的音频音，以便允许电视台检查颜色和音量），而且还要加入倒计时来引出片子的开始。

当剪辑师在编辑软件里处理音频的时候，他们必须用不同音量的叠加音频层来安排对白、音响效果和音乐，他们还需要调整音量的平衡来使每句对白都能听清楚，以及所有的音频都不失真。编辑软件还为剪辑师提供不同风格的转场效果。最好的转场是简单的切镜头和溶解。很多低成本动画最明显的特征是没法音画同步。剪辑师必须很小心地将音频与动画对位，这很值得花时间去做。

Unit 4　Produce an Animation Film
第 4 单元　制作动画电影

4.1　Getting Started
准备开始

Text

Before Starting the Project

How can you turn your ideas into a project? Elements such as character, setting, theme and story must all be considered before writing up the pitch materials. Follow these steps to develop your own project:

- Medium. Are you developing this idea mainly for TV, a film, a game, the Internet, an animation festival? What medium does your idea best suit?
- Demographics. Be sure you know who your target audience is. Will it appeal to a large enough audience? How can you make it appeal to an even wider demographic range?
- Format. The format selected for an animated project may be influenced by who will watch. There are six major types of formats an idea can be presented in, an animated feature film, Short Film, Television Special, an animated television series, webisodes (when seen on the Internet), and mobisodes (when seen on a mobile phone device).
- Core concept. What's the principal idea? Is this core idea going to be of utmost interest to your target audience? What else will the target audience like about your concept?
- Theme. Does it have a message or educational concept? Do you have a good tale to tell?
- Characters. Will they appeal to your specific audience? Can the audience identify with your characters? Are your characters archetypes?
- Design. The visual style. What's the look? Is it fresh?
- Setting and time period. Is this especially appealing? Why?
- Accessibility. Does it appeal to the needs, hopes, and dreams of your audience? Can your audience identify personally with your core concept?
- Freshness. Is this different enough from what's already out there?

Production Crew

Whether making a student film or a feature, the steps required to make and finish an animated film are pretty much the same. Making an animated film is not an easy task. You need to be organized and dedicated to completing it.

Crew sizes on independent projects tend to stay quite small. The benefit of being small is having more control over every aspect of your production. The problem with being small is that you are responsible for doing almost every aspect of your production. As productions get bigger, the different aspects of production are split between more people of different skills in order to spread the burden as well as get the job done more quickly.

Every production starts with a producer assembling a team. The producer is the person responsible for everything, and often holds the overall creative vision. The director will deal with the acting portion, the artistic and technical aspects of the film. Writers and storyboard artists create a story, while art directors and other artists are developing the look of the production and setting up characters, the backgrounds, the color palettes, and the props. When the story is locked, the dialogue is recorded, the animators work their magic. The compositors take all the backgrounds, characters, props, and effects and seamlessly blend them together with the proper camera moves. The editor takes all the composited scenes and dialogue and edits them together in the proper sequence, timing the edits such that the story flows with just the right timing. The sound designer builds and adds the sound effects, so that all are easily heard and understood. Finally, the project is delivered on film, video, the Internet, or some other medium.

Budget

Before you get too deep into production, you need to know what costs you're likely to run into, even when you are working on a project alone. When you produce animation for a client, you obviously need to create a budget to ensure, among other things, that you pay yourself and make a profit.

When you produce an independent project, you should make sure that you are prepared for all the expenses. For example, how much animation paper will be used, or even how long different people will work on any section of a project. Budgeting properly is an ability that comes with experience in the area of production. Tracking a budget during production and comparing it to your estimated budget, on the other hand, will help you understand actual costs.

Words and phrases

  theme　主题
  demographic　人群，人口统计学
  format　样式版式，设计，格式
  archetype　原型
  accessibility　可达性，可实现性
  freshness　新鲜度，创新
  burden　责任，负担

client 客户
animation festival 动画节
animated project 动画项目
animated feature film 动画电影，动画长片，时长为 90 分钟左右
short Film 短片
television special 专门在电视上播放的动画电影，不同于影院中播放的动画电影，时长为 30 分钟左右
animated television series 动画系列片，动画连续剧
webisode 网络视频短片
mobisode 手机视频短片
core concept 核心概念，核心理念
visual style 视觉风格
independent project 独立项目
storyboard artist 故事板（分镜头）艺术家，绘制故事板的人

Practice

1. Create three or four pieces of concept art that define the main shots and/or sequences in your film.

2. What's the producer's main task?

3. What should you do before starting an independent short film?

Further reading

Producing Independent 2D Character Animation: Making and Selling a Short Film
Editor: Mark Simon
Publisher: Focal Press (2003)

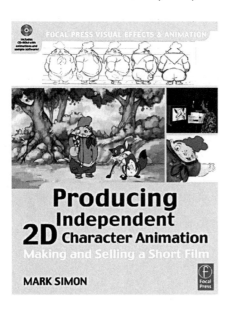

Web links

www.goldenagecartoons.com

Translation of text

在项目开始之前

如何才能把自己的创意做成一部动画？角色、背景、主题、故事等要素都要在编写汇总资料前考虑清楚。你可以按照下面的这些步骤来开发自己的动画项目：

- 媒体。你制作这部动画是为了电视节目、电影、游戏、网络还是参加动画节？你的想法最适合哪种媒体？
- 适合人群。要确定你的目标观众。这部动画会吸引足够多的观众么？该如何扩大这部片子的观众群？
- 规定样式。动画项目的样式选择取决于目标观众。有六种主要的样式类型可以实现你的创意，包括动画电影、短片、电视动画片、动画连续剧、网络动画以及手机动画。
- 核心概念。动画的主要想法是什么？目标观众会对它的核心理念感兴趣么？你的创意里还有什么其他内容会使目标观众喜欢？
- 主题。片子是有寓意的还是有教育意义的？将会讲述一个好的故事么？
- 角色。这些角色会吸引你的特定的观众么？观众会认同你的角色么？你的角色有原型么？
- 设计。片子的视觉风格是什么？看起来新颖么？
- 时代背景。这会特别有吸引力么？为什么？
- 可实现性。动画是否承载了观众的需求、希望和梦想？观众能否对你的想法感同身受？
- 创新。足够与众不同么？

创作团队

不论是制作学生动画作品还是动画电影，制作和完成动画电影所需的步骤几乎相同。制作动画电影不是一个容易的工作。你需要统筹安排并且全身心地投入来完成它。

独立动画项目的创作团队的规模通常比较小。规模小的好处是你可以很好地控制项目的每一个环节。但是问题是你必须得对项目的几乎每一个环节亲力亲为。做大项目时，各个环节的工作要分配给不同技能的人，以便分散工作量使工作快速完成。

每个项目都是由制片人来组建团队的。制片人是整个项目的负责人并控制片子整体的创意及视觉效果。导演负责表演部分，也就是动画的艺术和技术方面。作者和故事板艺术家负责设计故事情节，同时艺术指导和其他的工作人员负责片子的设定工作，如设定角色、背景、色彩调色板和道具。当故事情节确定、录制对白之后，动画师们也将开始他们的工作。合成师将所有的背景、角色、道具以及特效用适当的摄像机移动效果合成在一起。剪辑师将所有合成的场景和对话按照顺序和时间对位并剪切，这样故事情节就顺畅了。音响设计师负责加入音乐和声效，这样整个动画的效果就更好了。最后，片子将以电影、录像带、网络视频以及其他形式在媒体上播放。

预算

在开始项目之前，你必须得明确整个项目的花费，即使你是自己一个人完成一部动画也要这么做。

当为客户制作动画时，你显然要制订预算来确保自己的收入。

当你运作一个独立动画项目时，要确保你能承担所有费用。例如，会用到多少动画纸，或者每个环节的工作人员的工作时间有多长。合理地作预算是一种能力，这个能力是在工作中积累起来的。跟进一个项目的预算，然后与你估计的预算相比较，这样会帮助你了解项目真实的花销。

4.2 Animation Scriptwriting and Development
动画剧本写作及发展

Text

The Script

Usually animation begins with a script. If there is no script, then there is at least some kind of idea in written form—an outline or storyboard. When a premise is approved, it's expanded into an outline, and the outline is then expanded into a full script.

Where Do Ideas Come From?

Ideas can come from anywhere, so be open to all possibilities. Think about your own experiences, because this is what you know. How do you feel about the people in your life? Would any of them make good animation characters? Go back to your childhood. Maybe there are ideas there. What do you remember most? Why? What made you cry? Who were your best friends? How did you spend your summers? What were your dreams? What were the sights, sounds, and smells of your childhood? Use your emotions and all your senses. You might start the ideas flowing by photos, drawing or doodling. It could be easier for you to think visually. Don't be afraid to combine unrelated things from different drawings. Surf the Internet. What are the current trends? What's popular with kids now? Visit artists' websites for styles, and find something that interests you. Maybe there's a story to be developed there!

Mythology and fairy tales provide some great plots as well. Research a different period or culture. Make a list of quotations that can be used as themes. Buy a book and update or rewrite some of the stories, insert new characters, using a different location, or a different theme. Read comic books, science fiction, fantasy, and children's stories. Let those inform you and stimulate your imagination.

Let your imagination go wild. Brainstorm ideas with three columns:
- People or animals
- Places
- Things

Then you could pick one item at random from each column, juxtaposing and combining totally different ideas. You place the unexpected in an unexpected context and the obvious where it's least expected. You create surprising relationships. This is a great way to come up with original plots.

For example, what is that old man doing in the downtown with a purple balloon? You can use other combinations as well.

Developing Characters

Once past the brainstorming process, it's time to develop your characters. You'll want each of them to be as different from the others as possible. Those differences allow your characters to conflict and to relate to each other in funny ways. You'll probably want to start by writing a biography or fact sheet for each of your main characters. If you're an artist, you may prefer to start by drawing the characters. Usually writers choose to script scenes between characters to see how they'll react. You should give those characters a complete personality and an attitude toward each other. The more personality and individuality your characters have, the better your stories will be.

Character Profile

- Name (name may give us a clue)
- Sex
- Age
- Appearance (height; weight; hair color; eye color; physique; outstanding physical characteristics, such as dimples; dress)
- Movement
— How does he walk?
— Does he use expansive gestures when he talks?
- Voice (diction, vocabulary, power, pitch, unusual attributes)
— Give your character a dialogue tag.
— Make your character's voice distinctively.
- I.Q., abilities, talents, qualities (imagination, judgment)
- Personality/attitudes/temperament
— Is your character ambitious, loyal, sensitive? Inferior, optimistic? Shy? Sloppy? Eager?
— Character flaws, bad habits, weaknesses. Motivations, goals, ambitions. What does your character want?
- Values
— What's important to your character?

— How does he feel about the past or future? What in past situations have specifically affected the important choices he is making in this story?

- Situation

— What about his background or personality made him get involved?

— What kinds of changes has your character been going through?

- Ethnic background (when needed, research for authenticity) and any cultural baggage?
- Social/economic/political/cultural background and current status (research)
- Education
- Occupation(research well if he has one), values derived from the work.
- Lifestyle
- Family

— Parents? Husband or wife?

— How do these relationships now or in the past affect your character?

— How did he grow up? With love? Closeness? Neglect? Abuse?

- Hobbies, amusements

— What sports, exercise, or hobbies does your character engage in?

— What does he do on Saturdays? Sundays? Tuesday evenings?

- Era—if this is historical, research well.
- Setting or place

— How would your character react to this setting? Would he be happy here?

— What sounds, smells, and tastes are in your character's surroundings?

You don't need to answer every single one of these questions. Not every question will be applicable or necessary for each character you develop. But do take the time to get to know your character. Use the Character Profile to help you explore personality. Different kinds of stories have different kinds of characters. The most important information is what will help you delve into the thoughts, feelings, and emotions of your characters. Feelings and emotions are keys to good writing! You might even want to write down your own character profile and delve more deeply into the things that make you tick. Your characters should be allowed some room to grow as you write more about them. The more you know about your characters, the better.

Story Theme

The theme is the central values of the story. A theme is something for the audience to think about later. It gives the story some substance. It's an observation about life and the people in our world, and helps us understand each other and the world around us. All stories can be broken down to only three types: Man vs. God (or nature), Man vs. Man, and Man vs. Himself.

Love, friendship, family, etc. Universal and timeless themes that touch us all are usually the best themes for films. Character, plot, and theme are all connected. A theme is felt, not indoctrinated or preached. We want characters show their value in life by the actions, and fight for what is good in the world. Values are expressed mostly through action. Conflict and opposing values are at the heart of any story.

Basic Animation Scriptwriting Structure

Structure exists to help you write a better story, but differences in the length of your story make a difference in the complexity of your structure. Differences in type (feature, kid's cartoon, Internet short) or genre (action/adventure, comedy, preschool) can also make a difference in complexity and style. A feature script is longer and requires more structure to hold our interest. An Internet short or one-minute TV cartoon requires very little plot. Generally action/adventure shows require more plot than gag-driven comedy shows. Prime-time animated shows generally use a sitcom structure with more clever dialogue and less action.

All stories must have a beginning, middle, and end. A short series script (for TV or the Internet) must be about the protagonist of that series and be centered on them. The protagonist of each episode must have a goal or motive, and someone or something must oppose that goal. These are the basic story musts, and the same applies to a film. Of course, there are also independent animated films that are more abstract and make no attempt at telling a tale.

Normally scripts use a three-act structure:

- Act I This ends after the problem has been set up. (The young man is on top of a flagpole.)
- Act II This ends before the climax. (Someone is pelting him with squishy tomatoes and rotten oranges.)
- Act III Resolution. (He finds a way to get down.)

Occasionally a TV animation script will be written in just two acts, but even with only two acts, the basic three-act structure will be spread out over the length of those two acts. The three acts of a typical television script may be about the same length, although the last act will probably be the shortest. Sometimes the first act is shorter. A three-act feature script will probably have acts that are apportioned: 25 percent for Act I, 50 percent for Act II, and 25 percent for Act III. The rules are not carved in stone.

Creating the Story

This is a simple step-by-step method for creating a story:

- Who is your protagonist, star, or hero for this episode? Protagonist is the person who drives the story. What is the protagonist's character flaw, fault, or weakness? How does this flaw hurt or annoy others?
- Go to the end of your story. What does this character learn about himself and how to treat others by the end of this episode? What was the lesson that the story taught him—the theme of your story?
- Back to the beginning. What does your protagonist want? This goal should start low and snowball throughout the story until it's almost an obsession by the end.

- Who (what villain or opponent) can best attack the protagonist's character flaw, oppose his values, and try to stop him from reaching his goal? This villain should ideally want the same thing as the protagonist.
- What's the catalyst or inciting incident, the person or thing from the outside, that causes the protagonist to come up with his goal and start the story moving? It may be the villain that puts the story into action, especially in a mystery.
- Make sure that all story points are related and tied together so that you're telling only one story.
- Your protagonist develops a game plan to reach his goal. The villain attacks over and over. There is usually a major reversal or turning point in the way that the action is going at the end of Act I, spinning the action around in another direction.
- In Act II new information is coming out. Your protagonist keeps revising his plan because it's not working. A high point is likely about halfway through the script. Everything looks good for your protagonist, and it appears that he'll attain his goal. But your protagonist has a defeat or apparent defeat, giving the villain or antagonist an advantage. This starts the downward slide for your protagonist.
- There's another turning point toward the end of Act II, spinning the action around again.
- The major crisis is the lowest point in the story for your protagonist. It's the reverse of what your protagonist wants. Often it's here that he's faced with his critical choice. This crisis might be the turning point at the end of Act II, but it can't come too soon or the third act will drag. If the major crisis is at the end of Act II, it requires a short third act.
- In Act III your protagonist comes back and tries harder. This is the biggest battle. It's best when it's a physical battle and a battle of values. Your protagonist wins! This is the climax! Everything must build to this point.
- Resolution. Wrap up quickly.

This method works best for longer material: a feature or an hour or at least a half-hour story. It works best when you want more character, more plot, and less belly laughs. The steps are general, a structure to work toward. Your story may be slightly different.

Words and phrases

sight　风景，视野
surf the internet　上网
current trends　当代动向，目前的趋势
mythology　神话
quotation　引文，引用语
science fiction　科幻小说，科幻电影
brainstorm　头脑风暴，集思广益
column　列，专栏

juxtapose 并列，并置
merry-go-round 旋转木马
conflict 冲突，矛盾
biography 传记，自传
fact sheet 情况说明书，资料简报，专题介绍单
diction 措辞，用语
temperament 气质，性情，性格
optimistic 乐观的
sloppy 马虎的，粗心的
eager 热心的
character flaw 角色缺陷，性格缺陷
ethnic background 种族背景
amusement 消遣，娱乐，乐趣
character profile 角色简介
indoctrinated 被灌输的
preach 说教，鼓吹
prime-time 黄金时段
sitcom（situation comedy） 情景喜剧
protagonist 主角，主人公，主演
episode 插曲，一段情节，有趣的事件
villain 坏人，反派角色
opponent 对手，敌人
catalyst 催化剂，刺激因素
inciting 煽动的，刺激的
turning point 转折点，转机
antagonist 对立面，反面人物
crisis 危机
wrap up 整理，收拾，完成

Practice

1. What is the basic structure of a film? Explain the three-act structure.
2. How do you understand the story theme?
3. What is a character profile? Create a character profile for your own script.

Translate into English

1. 主题是需要感受出来的，不是靠灌输和说教，是观众看后会思考的东西，是对我们所生活的世界和人的观察。
2. 一部电影的剧本通常比较长，并且需要很多的情节结构来吸引观众。

Further reading

Animation Writing and Development: From Script Development to Pitch
Editor: Jean Ann Wright
Publisher: Focal Press (2005)

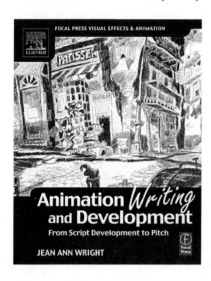

Web links

www.thescreenplaywriters.com

Translation of text

剧本

通常动画制作都是从剧本开始的。如果没有剧本,也至少要有文字形式的东西——故事大纲或者是故事板。当一个故事的前提设定通过后,要将它扩展成故事大纲,接着大纲就可以扩展成一个完整的剧本。

灵感从何而来?

灵感可以从任何地方得来,所以对任何可能性要有一个开放的心态。想想你自己的亲身经历,因为这些是你所知道的。你对生活里的其他人有什么感觉?他们当中有没有合适的人选可以变成动画角色?你可以回想你的童年来找到些素材。什么让你记忆深刻?为什么?什么东西把你弄哭了?你曾经最好的朋友是谁?你都怎么过暑假?你的梦想是什么?你的童年有没有什么特别的景象、声音和味道?把你的情感和所有感官都用上。你可以通过照片、图画和涂鸦来构思。通过视觉来想象会比较容易。不要害怕把不同图画里无关的东西联想起来。上网看看当前的流行趋势。最受孩子们欢迎的是什么?通过访问艺术家的网站来收集艺术风格,找到让你感兴趣的东西。或许这里正有一个故事有待展现!

神话和童话故事也可以提供很多精彩的情节。必要的时候要研究不同时代的文化。将可用做故事主题的事件列一个单子。买一本书,更新或者重写其中的一些故事,加入新的角色、不同的场景或者不同的主题。也可以多看看漫画书、科幻小说和儿童故事,让这些东西来激发你的想象力。

放开你的想象力，你可以用以下内容的三个列表来做头脑风暴：
- 人物或者动物
- 地点
- 事件

然后你可以从各个列表中随机选择一个放在一起，并将不同的内容结合起来。你会发现它们之间的关系完全是意想不到。你创造出了一种新奇的关系。这是一种从独特情节开始构思故事的好方法。例如，一个老人在闹市区带着一个紫色气球能做什么呢？你也可以用其他的组合来尝试。

进一步发展角色

一旦通过头脑风暴环节，接下来就该扩展角色了。你一定希望每个角色都与众不同。这些差异可以让角色之间用一种有趣的方式相互冲突或者关联。你应该从为每一个主要角色写传记或者个人说明开始。如果你是一个画家，你或许喜欢从绘制角色开始。通常作者选择从角色之间的情节开始写，以此来看角色之间是如何互动的。你的角色个性越鲜明，故事会写得越有意思。

角色资料

- 姓名（姓名会给我们一定的线索）
- 性别
- 年龄
- 外貌（身高、体重、头发的颜色、眼睛的颜色、体型，以及明显的身体特征如酒窝、衣着）
- 动作特征

他走路是什么样子？
当他说话的时候用夸张的姿态么？

- 声音（用语、词汇、强度、音高、不寻常的特点）

给你的角色设计口头禅。
让你的角色的声音独特。

- 智商、能力、才华、素质（想象力、判断力）
- 个性、态度、气质

你的角色是有事业心的、忠诚的，敏感的么？自卑还是乐观？害羞？马虎？热心吗？
性格上的缺陷，不良的生活习惯，弱点。动机，目标，抱负。什么是你的角色想要的？

- 价值观

对你的角色来说什么是最重要的？
对于过去和未来，他有什么样的感觉？在故事里曾经发生过什么特别的事情对他的抉择产生重要的影响？

- 处境

是什么样的背景或个性使他介入到这件事情中来?
你的角色正在经历什么样的转变?
- 种族背景（如果需要，要研究其真实性）和信仰
- 社会/经济/政治/文化背景和当前的状态（需要研究）
- 教育程度
- 职业（如果他有职业的话要仔细调查），从工作中获得的价值观。
- 生活方式
- 家庭

父母是什么样的？丈夫或妻子是什么样的？
现在或过去与家人的关系对你的角色有什么样的影响？
他是如何成长的？被关爱的？自闭的？被忽视的？被虐待的？
- 爱好、娱乐方式

你的角色平时参加什么样的体育项目、运动，或者有什么爱好？
他每周六都做什么？周日呢？周二晚上呢？
- 生活的年代——如果他是个历史人物就需要仔细研究调查。
- 场景或地点

你的角色对这个场景会作何反应？在这他会高兴么？
在你的角色周围有什么声音、味道？

你不需要回答以上的全部问题。不是每一个问题对角色的扩展都很适用或很必要。但是你一定要花时间来了解你的角色。用角色简介的方法帮助你扩展角色性格。不同的故事里会有不同的角色。最重要的资料会帮助你深入到角色的思想、感受和情感。感觉和情感是写出好故事的关键。你应该写下你自己的角色简介并且对你的选项进行深入的剖析。当你在描写角色时，应该给他们一定的成长空间。你对角色了解得越多越好。

故事主题

主题是故事的核心价值。所谓主题就是观众看后会思考的东西。它给予故事一些实质性的东西，是对我们所生活的世界和人的观察，并帮助我们了解彼此，了解我们周围的事件。所有的故事可以分成三大类：人与神（或大自然）、人与他人、人与自己。

爱情、友谊、亲情等，这些普遍和永恒的主题通常是触动我们最好的电影主题。角色、情节和主题需要被串联在一起。主题是需要感受出来的，不是靠灌输和说教。我们要让角色通过他们的行动以及为了美好事物的不断奋斗来体现他们生活中的价值观。价值观通常是通过行动来表现的。冲突及对立的价值观是所有故事要表达的重点。

动画剧本的基本写作结构

结构的存在是为了帮助你写出更好的故事，但是故事的长度不同会让结构的复杂性也不相同。类型不同（动画电影长片、儿童卡通、网络短片）或流派不同（动作/冒险类、喜剧类、针对学龄前儿童的动画）也会使复杂性和风格不同。一部剧本比较长的电影就需要更多的结构来吸引我们。而网络短片或者

一分钟的电视卡通节目则需要非常少的情节。总的来说动作/冒险类的节目所需要的情节要多于搞笑的喜剧类的节目。黄金时段的动画节目一般都像情景喜剧一样，采用机智的对话和较少的动作的方式。

所有的故事必须有一个开头、中间和结尾。系列短片的剧本（电视或网络）必须以主人公为中心来写。每集的主人公必须有一个目标或者动机，同时一些人或一些事必须反对这个目标。这些是故事里的基本要素，也同样适用于动画电影。当然，也有很多独立动画电影非常抽象，没有试图讲述一个故事。

常用的三幕剧本结构：

- 第一幕，问题出现之后这一幕结束。（有个年轻人在旗杆的顶端。）
- 第二幕，高潮出现后这一幕结束。（有人向他投掷黏糊糊的西红柿和烂橘子。）
- 第三幕，解决。（他找到方法下来。）

偶尔电视动画剧本只会用两幕，但即使只有两幕，基本的三幕结构也会被展开成两幕的长度。标准的电视动画剧本的三幕长度基本上是一样的，尽管最后一幕很有可能会最短。有的时候第一幕也会比较短。三幕式的电影剧本可能会有这样的比例安排：第一幕占25%，第二幕占50%，第三幕占25%。当然这些不是一定的。

构思故事

这是一个简单的一步一步来构思故事的方法：

- 在这一集里谁是你的主人公、明星或英雄？主人公是驱动故事的人。主人公的缺点、过错、弱点是什么？这些问题是怎么伤害或烦扰到别人的？
- 到故事的结尾。角色学到了什么，在这一集的结尾他是如何对待其他人的？这个故事给他上了怎样的一课？也就是故事的主题是什么？
- 回到故事的开头。主人公想要什么？目标的起点应该较低，然后像雪球一样随着情节发展越滚越大，直到结尾的时候几乎是一个大难题。
- 谁（坏人或对手）能攻击主人公的缺点，反对他的价值观，并试图阻止他达到目标呢？理想情况下这个坏人应该和主人公想得到同一件东西。
- 外部的人或事物，哪些催化剂或煽动事件导致主角向目标迈进并开始展开故事情节？很可能是坏人来推动情节发展，尤其是使故事越来越复杂。
- 要确保所有的故事点都是相关联并紧密联系在一起的，这样就是在讲述一个完整的故事。
- 主人公制订了一个计划来达到自己的目标。坏人一遍又一遍地攻击。通常在第一幕要结束的时候有一个大逆转或转折点，使故事情节转向另外一个方向发展。
- 在第二幕，新的情况会出现。主人公会不断修改他的计划。故事最精彩的部分大概在剧本一半的位置。一切看起来都有利于主人公，而且他马上就要达到自己的目标了。但是主人公出现了一个挫折或者是表面上的挫折，让坏人或对手占了上风。主人公开始走下坡路。
- 接近第二幕结尾的时候会出现另一个转折点，再次将剧情领向另一个方向。
- 主人公的重大危机是故事的最低点，这与主人公所想要达到的目标是相反的。通常在这个时候他要面临着关键的抉择。这个危机可能是第二幕结尾时的转折点，但它不能来得太早或者第三幕要推后一些。如果重大危机发生在第二幕结尾，则需要第三幕短一些。
- 在第三幕，主人公卷土重来并且更加努力。这是最大的一场争斗。最好是身体与价值观的争斗并存。主人公赢了！这就是故事的高潮！一切都必须为了这一点而设计。

- 解决问题。快速结束。

这个方法对于较长的片子效果比较好：适用于一个小时的动画电影或者至少半个小时的故事。当你想要更多角色、更多情节和较少笑点的时候，这个方法最有效。这是编写剧本的一般步骤，以此作为编写结构，你的故事或许会略有不同。

4.3 Character Design
角色设定

Text

Before storyboarding, we need to know what the character looks like. We will, however, often work on both storyboarding and design at the same time as we determine what we want the character to look like. We then finalize the storyboards with the approved character design. Here are a few guidelines that can make you design better characters.

Style

The first thing you need to consider is style. With your concept art you should already have, it is time to hone in on the precise look for design. Style is infinite in its conception. Do you want your film in its approach to be traditional cartoon, wild and wacky contemporary cartoon, photorealistic, etc.? All these things have to be thought through at this stage.

Look at your favorite character designs to guide you, to help you decide what area you want to concentrate your design thinking toward. Don't copy them, just use them for inspiration and direction only. Narrow it down to exactly what things you like and what things you don't like about your character ideas. If you have a favorite cartoon or illustration style, begin to redraw your character roughs in that style. As previously suggested, don't copy the original characters; just use them for their style approach. Try to analyze the way they are drawn and their inherent simplicity or otherwise, and try to emulate that with what you are trying to create with your own ideas.

Another thing you most likely don't want to do is have a character design style that is very dissimilar from your background or environment style. You'll want a compatible style throughout. But animation is capable of anything, so don't entirely close off all your options at this stage. Don't forget, that using a rounded, curvilinear style of line approach will give you a softer, cuter style of character. Angular, rectilinear line and form will give a more aggressive, hard-cut style of character. Similarly, with the colors you use, genetically pastel shades imply a softer, cuter style, whereas pure primary colors suggest a wacky kind of personality.

Personality

Next, think about the kind of personality your character will have. Is he or she friendly, aggressive, dumb, bright, laid back, uptight, attractive, ugly, whatever? So much of the personality of a character defines the design style. Think carefully about the shape and the style that you give your character, as the form and nature of the drawing will determine how the audiences perceive him or her.

Sketches

With all these thoughts in mind, it is time to start your character design. Character design normally starts with a series of sketches. First, rough draw your thoughts as quick thumbnail sketches. Get as many ideas and approaches down as you can. It may take dozens, or hundreds, of drawings to work out the subtleties of a character. We will often work from silhouettes to come up with a general form for our character. Remember, characters are seldom alone, and they need to work with other characters. Animated motion tests may also help determine the look of a character. Even show your initial and development sketches to others for feedback. What they think the inherent personalities and attitudes your characters have.

Proportion

Once you have established the general characteristics of your character, begin to focus down by better defining his or her key essentials. Does the bigger nose really make him or her better? Would the character work better thinner, fatter, or more buff? And so on. Ask yourself these questions about all aspects of your character. The proportion of your character says so much about him or her. The short character with a big head is much more likely to convince us that he or she is bright and intelligent.

Be aware of head heights. Head heights define just how tall your character is and what size the character's head is in relation to his or her body. The more cartoonish your character design style, the less head height he or she is likely to contain. Typically, the head height of a character is calculated by the number of times his or her head divides into the overall height. Human head height measurement is usually defined as seven. With Manga characters it can be as much as nine, but in the simplest of cartoon characters it can be as low as two. The head height of a character will therefore define how realistic or cartoonish he or she appears to be.

Detail

Now, it's time to further develop the character. Elements to watch for in character design include not only the ones that enhance or hurt the look of the character, but also those that affect the animation process. Remember, especially if you are a 2D animator, that every line that you put into a character design has to be redrawn 24 times a second (or 12 if you are animating on two's)! Small details may be too hard to animate. Details such as shaggy fur, spots and speckles, scales, and fabric designs may look great in sketches, but animators have to be able to duplicate such details in a timely and accurate manner. Loose clothing may have to have a lot of animated follow-through. High-budget animation makes good use of flowing cloth and hair, but low-budget animation needs to stay away from too much secondary animated motion because it increases the number of drawings that must be done. So try to create your character with the least amount of detail and texture that you can get away with. You will most definitely thank yourself for doing this when you reach the animation stage later on!

Expression Sheet

Once a drawing of a character is approved, you will start working out expressions. Expressions are drawings of a character expressing different emotional behaviors, such as crying, laughing, yelling, being sneaky, and many others. Capturing the proper expressions for a character is important. Since characters usually have more than one facial expression, we need to have a sampling of various expressions. A sheet of expressions guides animators in how characters react to things so that characters will look consistent throughout the animation process. As we go through the expressions, we revise how they should look and toss out the ones that don't seem to fit his character.

Phonemes, or the different mouth shapes needed for each sound, will also need to be designed. Different styles of animation often draw mouth shapes in different ways. Each character needs a defined set of mouth positions so that it will be consistent.

Turn-around

The turn-around is one of the most important parts of the character design. It shows the character from every conceivable angle and finalizes all details and maintains a consistent look for the character as he moves. Therefore, draw the character from the front, side, and perhaps a three-quarter and rear view. A comprehensively planned and drawn model sheet will solve all these problems for you long before you begin the real challenge of animating the character.

If you have more than one animator working on a character, it is also important to do constructions. Constructions break a character down into simple shapes to help speed up rough animation and, again, to help maintain the consistent look of the character.

If you are designing a character who will be modeled in three dimensions later, you will most likely need to design your character in the classical arms up, "crucifix" mode.

Color

The final step in character design is color. Color design needs to work on the character as well as with the other characters and the backgrounds. When the script calls for dark shots, there will also be a set of night colors for each character.

Lastly, in order to solve all the issues related to your final character design, you will now need to color your model sheet so that you know exactly how many, and what, colors your design needs to contain. Again, you will need to make sure that the colors selected work well with the color schemes and painting techniques depicted in your background or environment art style, as envisioned in your concept art.

Words and phrases

guideline   指南，指导方针

inspiration 灵感
inherent 固有的，内在的
compatible 兼容的，能共处的
curvilinear 曲线的，由曲线组成的
angular 有角的，生硬的
rectilinear 直线的
hard-cut style 硬切风格
pastel shade 轻淡优美的色彩，粉彩，淡色
uptight 紧张的，心情焦躁的
thumbnail 缩略图
subtlety 微妙之处，细微的差别
proportion 比例，部分
shaggy 蓬松的，表面粗糙的
speckle （皮肤、羽毛等上的）斑点，斑纹
fabric 面料，布料
duplicate 复制
expression sheet 表情图
phoneme 音位，音素
turn-around 转面
three-quarter view 四分之三侧视
rear view 后视图，背视图
comprehensively 全面地，综合地，包括地
crucifix 十字架，双手平举
envision 想象，预想

Practice

1. Explain the step-by-step method for character design.
2. How to establish the general characteristics of a character?

Translate into English

1. 转面图是角色设计的步骤之一，它从各个角度来展示角色并确保角色在运动的时候不会变形。
2. 根据你喜欢的角色设计来引导你的设计思路，不要复制他们，只需要把它们用做灵感来源和设计方向。

Further reading

The Art of Madagascar: Escape 2 Africa
Editor: Jerry Beck
Publisher: Insight Editions (2008)

Web links

www.characterdesign.blogspot.com

Translation of text

在绘制故事板之前，我们需要知道角色长什么样子。不过，当我们需要确定角色形象的时候，也经常同时绘制故事板和进行角色设计。然后我们用已经通过的角色设计来完成故事板。这里有一些方法指导可以让你设计出更好的角色。

风格

你需要考虑的第一件事是风格。将已有的概念设计继续加工修改成精准的设计稿。风格是无限的。你希望动画是传统卡通风格的，还是狂野、古怪的当代卡通风格，还是写实逼真的风格呢？所有的这些事情都要在这个阶段考虑清楚。

根据你喜欢的角色设计来引导你的设计思路。不要复制他们，只需要把它们用做灵感来源和设计方向。你对角色的想法要确切到哪些是你喜欢的、哪些是你不喜欢的。如果你有一个特别喜欢的卡通风格或插图风格，可以按照这些风格来绘制角色草稿。就像之前建议的，不要复制原角色，只需要用它们的设计风格。试着分析它们绘制的方法和内在的规律，以及试着通过模仿它们来做自己的角色设计。

另一件要注意的事是不要让你的角色设计风格与背景或环境风格差别太大。整个片子的风格要协调。但是动画是无所不能的，所以在这个阶段不要做最后的定论。不要忘了，使用圆润的曲线风格会给你一个柔和、可爱的角色。有棱角的直线风格会给你一个凌厉的角色。同样，根据你所用的颜色，通常淡雅的色调意味着温和、可爱的风格，反之纯粹的原色显示出一种古怪的性格。

个性

接下来，要考虑角色的个性是什么样的。他或她是友善的、凌厉的、沉默寡言的、活泼的、随和的、易怒的、有魅力的、丑陋的，或者是其他什么样的？一个角色需要如此多的性格特征来明确其设计风格。仔细思考给角色什么样的形状和形式，因为形式和图形的本质将决定观众是如何理解角色的。

素描稿

带着所有的这些问题，我们开始设计角色。角色设计通常从一系列的素描稿开始。首先，简略快速地画一些素描小稿。尽可能地把你所有的想法都画出来。可能要有几十或几百张这样的图稿才能确定出角色的所有细节。我们经常从剪影轮廓入手来确定角色大概的形体。记住，角色很少是单独的，他们需要和其他角色一起来设计。动画的动作测试也可以帮助确定角色的设计。你甚至可以把最初的草稿和改进的设计稿给别人看，看他们的反馈意见。看看他们怎么看待角色内在的个性和态度。

比例

角色的一般特征确定好之后，就要开始关注确定角色设计的关键要素。大一些的鼻子会不会让他或她看起来更好？角色如果瘦点、胖点或强壮点会不会好些？关于角色的所有方面你要反复地问自己这些问题。角色的比例有很多的含义。一个矮个子却有着大脑袋的角色极有可能让我们相信他或她既聪明又机智。

要注意角色头高。头高决定了角色的身高以及头身比例。你的角色风格越卡通，头高就越小。通常，角色的头高是通过总身高与头部的倍数来计算的。人类的头身比例通常为1∶7，日本漫画角色会高达1∶9，而最简单的卡通角色会低到1∶2。因此头高会决定角色是写实风格的还是卡通风格的。

细节

现在要进一步地扩展角色。在角色设计里要注意不仅包括会增强或损害角色形象的元素，也包括会影响动画制作过程的元素。要记住，尤其如果你是二维动画师，在角色设计里添加的每一条线都将要一秒重画24次（如果你用一拍二的话就是12次）。小细节很难做动画。像毛茸茸的皮毛、斑点和斑纹、鳞片以及布料这样的细节在设计稿里会很好看，但是动画师不得不及时、准确地重复这些细节。宽松的衣服可能会有很多跟随动画。高预算的动画项目会给衣服和头发做很好的动画，但是低成本的动画项目会尽量避免过多的二级动画动作，因为这样会增加工作量。所以对角色设计尽量用最少的细节和纹理。当你进行到动画阶段的时候你会感谢自己当初的决定。

表情图

角色设计通过后，你就要开始设计表情。表情就是角色表现出来的不同的情绪性行为，比如像哭、笑、喊叫、鬼鬼祟祟及其他。捕捉到角色恰当的表情是很重要的。由于一个角色通常有许多面部表情，我们需要采集各种各样的表情。表情图可以在动画制作过程中告诉动画师角色对事物的反应是什么样的。当我们在检查表情图的时候，要修改成他们应该有的表情并且删掉那些不适合角色的表情。

每个声音的音位或者不同的口型也需要设计出来。不同风格的动画口型的绘制方法也是不同的。每一个角色都需要一套设计好的嘴部位置，这样在整部片子里他们的口型将是一致的。

转面图

转面图是角色设计最重要部分之一。它从每一个可能的角度来展示角色并确定了所有的细节，使角色在运动的时候保持一致的形象而不会变形。因此，要从正面、侧面、四分之三侧面和背面来画角色。一个全面计划好并画好的模型图将在你真正开始挑战角色动画之前解决所有的问题。

如果有多位动画师来绘制同一个角色，做解构就很重要。解构就是将一个角色打破分成许多简单的形状来帮助加速完成动画草稿，以及帮助动画师保持角色造型一致。

如果你正在设计的角色将要在三维软件里建模,你就需要把角色设计成经典的手臂平举的"十字架"模式。

色彩

角色设计的最后一个步骤是色彩。色彩设计需要将角色的色彩和其他角色及背景的色彩放在一起设计。如果剧本里有黑暗的镜头,将需要为每一个角色设计一套夜间色彩。

最后,为了解决关于最终角色设计的所有问题,你需要给模型图上色,这样你就可以确切地知道你的设计到底需要含有多少以及什么样的色彩。同样,你也需要确定所选择的色彩与配色方案,并确保针对背景和环境艺术风格的绘画技法都很协调,就像在概念设计里期望的那样。

4.4 Camera Language and the Storyboard
镜头语言与故事板

Text

Camera Shots

Good storyboards contain a variety of shots, and the lengths of scenes vary. Tension is built with mood and atmosphere, with composition, or with shots. Artists change camera angles to present different perspectives, determine the best angles for each shot and show the audience all that you want them to see. Camera angles are a critical way to keep the audience interested in the story you are telling – imagine if you saw only one point of view for an entire movie.

(1) Shot Angles
- Extreme Close-Up (EXT CU): so close you see only figure's eyes, mouth, necklace, etc.
- Close-Up (CU): shoulder to head, subtle facial acting is used or small details to be noticed. Just don't overuse them.
- Medium Shot (MS): about waist length, used when the characters become more important than the surroundings. Shows facial expressions and gestures.
- Medium Long Shot: cuts the figure just above the knees.
- Long Shot (also Establishing Shot): any shot that holds a full length figures, or objects in the distance (background).
- Far Shot
- Extreme Far
- Wide Shot: shows the placement of the figure for the audience.
- Upshot
- Downshot
- Over the shoulder (OTS) point of view: puts focus on the character facing camera, yet still subconsciously includes the other character.

(2) Camera Moves on a Board
- Panoramic (Pan): the camera moves horizontally to take in a panoramic scene. If the acting changes through the pan, show a few of the poses.

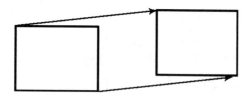

Arrows Show the direction of the pan, A is the start point, B is the stop point.

- Track-in/Track-out: the camera moves smoothly on a track to capture the movement in the scene.

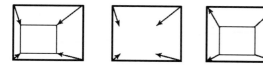

Track-in/ Track-out also called Push in/ Push out, Slow in/ Slow out.

- Zoom Shot: the focus goes from wide angle to CU with a zoom lens.
- Camera Adjust: the camera moves less than one full frame in any direction. Only show the entire frame of the stop point.

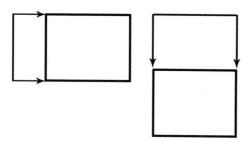

Arrows drawn from one frame to another.

(3) Transitions

One of the most important jobs of a good storyboard artist is to create smooth transitions between scenes. Scenes must hook up to the scene preceding and the one following. Don't just cut to the next scene, transitions must be made creatively, make sure the flow is maintained, and we move into a new scene naturally.

Before each transition storyboard artists write one of the following:
- Fade in: A camera function. Opening the aperture from 0% to 100% exposure, over a number of

frames. (Starts dark and gets bright)
- Fade out: A camera function. Closing the aperture from 100% to 0% exposure, over a number of frames. (Starts bright and gets dark)
- Cut: A term used to describe an end to the current scene. The next scene consists of a different location or angle that is separate from the previous scene. (The end of the scene)
- Cross dissolve: A combination of fade out and fade in produces a "ghost-like" effect as one scene disappears while the other appears at the same time. Start and Stop frame are the same for both the fade out and fade in.

Thinking Like a Camera Sees

The best storyboard artists will think like a camera sees, consider shot angle in any scene, and whether the mood requires a camera move. Do we need to see a prop in close up because the prop is an important story point? Do we need to see how someone reacts? Don't overuse pan shots, track-ins, or track-outs. When tracks and pans are used, keep them simple. Producers of CG animation usually encourage sweeping camera moves. In either traditional or CG animation, slow truck-ins with cross dissolves give the impression of multiplane moves.

(1) Angles Tell Story

Here are different shot angles for the same scene. The first drawing shows three planes in the background, but the two people are standing exactly next to one another, that is too flat and uninspired. The second drawing is more dynamic. The young man is closer creating depth. He is placed higher in the frame than the old man, subconsciously making the man more important. In the last drawing, the young man is almost on top of us. It is very dynamic, but remember that, save it for the scenes that call for it.

A is boring, B is better, C is very dynamic, but don't over use it.

(2) Horizon Line

Think about each scene and what it's really about. Appropriate use of a horizontal line will enhance the power. The first drawing is a mundane shot, and the lawyers seem to be standing the same distance from the camera as the judge is in his seat. The second drawing is a more dramatic shot. The difference is subtle. But this revision focus on the judge, plus adds drama with an upshot on him. Now the judge holds more power, and the distance between the lawyers and him is emphasized. All thanks to lowering the horizon.

Appropriate use of a horizontal line will enhance the power.

(3) Upshots and Downshots

Most shots are straight on, upshots and downshots add variety and drama to scenes. Upshots place the audience beneath the focus and downshots place the audience above.

(4) Screen Direction: Staying on the Good Side of the Camera Line

The imaginary camera never crosses an imaginary action axis by turning more than ninety degrees. That disorients the audience. Even close ups of two people talking are staged with less than a ninety-degree cross between the two matched close ups. The camera setup at the bottom of the picture is correct. The camera setup on another side would disorient us as we cut back and forth between shots. Images should be drawn as if the cameras stay on the same side of the axis.

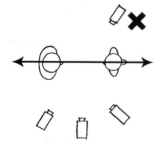  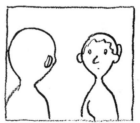 

Keeping the camera from jumping the camera line is the easiest thing to learn, easiest mistake to spot. But is still the most common mistake board artists make.

（5）Screen Direction: Staying on the Same Side of the Screen

Keep the cutting clean by keeping the characters in the same relative space in sequential shots. It's just as helpful in keeping things clear in your staging and storytelling.

（6）Screen Direction: Continuity in Moving Directions

We're conditioned to moving our eyes left to right when reading, so left to right is more natural to the eyes. We need to keep some space in front of the car or character in the direction they're moving, the audience subconsciously needs to feel the character has some place to go.

 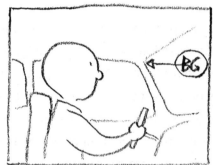 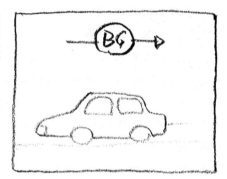

The car is moving left to right shown by the arrow calling for the background (BG) to pan behind the car from right to left.

（7）Inserts

Full screen close ups of actions, objects, text, or character's reactions placed as if inserted over a longer scene, or over another character's dialogue. When you choose your shots, think in terms of both the dramatic impact on the audience, and visual variety.

Practice

We break down the scene into the basic shots before adding rough sketches. For example, a man standing on a fence, this may show the whole person and the whole fence. That's called a long shot. If you want to see what the man is holding up to his ear, we cut to a close up, and he has a little box by his ear. Some arrows may show that the man is shaking the box back and forth. Then we cut back to the long shot, and we see a girl pulling a wagon. If we want to see what's in the wagon, from the perspective of the man on the fence. We have a downward angle, a Spiderman point of view. We can cut closer, and see that in the bowl is a goldfish. Pull it back to the shot where the girl pulling the wagon is talking to the man on the fence. To see from the girl's perspective, we have an upward angle. It's an imposing shot, like looking up at a monument, or a giant. As he hands the box to the girl, we can shift to a side view, so you can see from the profile that they exchange the box. It makes us want to know what's in the box, to explore the relationship, to see what will happen next.

The Storyboard

After the scriptwriting, the most important part of the development is the storyboard. The script is the words, and the storyboard translates the script to life in a succession of rectangular sketches, using a camera view. Storyboards must have clear visuals to explain what the scene, or even entire board is about. It is much like a very detailed comic book. This visual tool of storytelling, the storyboard, gives you a chance to state your ideas.

The storyboard will show all the scenes, to explain to everyone, from the animators to the director and producer, how the story works. All your scenes, a sequential visual plan of major actions, camera positions, angles and shots have to be determined before you commit to commencing the expensive and lengthy animation process.

(1) Format of Storyboard

How you make your storyboards is up to you. The basic concept of storyboards is to tell the story with pictures and words, incorporating direction, sound and dialogue instructions. Some people prefer to board in the normal horizontal storyboard format. Another approach to storyboard layout is the three-column format, one column for notes and directions, one for the images, and one for the dialogue. This is a very good systematic method that works well in conjunction with the X-sheet. Whichever way you choose, keep the drawings simple, with one for each shot or key frame. You may want to add visual markers for camera movements such as pans, tracks or zoom.

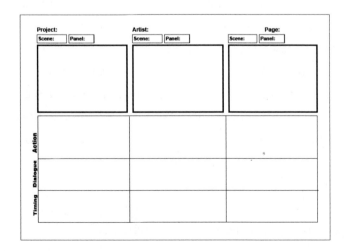

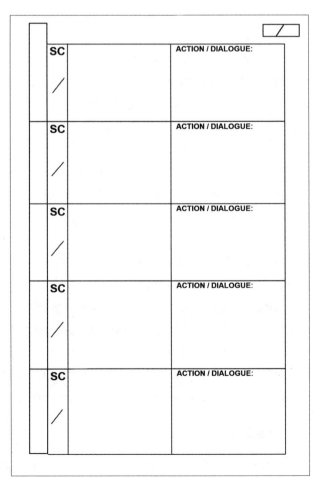

(2) Building the Storyboard

Let's start now to place characters inside the individual rectangular frames that make up the shots. To devise a good storyboard, ask yourself the following questions:

- What is the story about?
- Who are the characters? What do they do and say?
- Which characters are in the foreground, middle ground, and background?
- Are they in conflict and with whom?
- Where does the conflict take place?
- When are long, medium and close-up shots necessary?

The answers to all these questions become clear when illustrated in the storyboard. The artist reads the script to familiarize himself with plot and characters and their personalities. Then he looks at model sheets, available backgrounds, and any stock animation. He determines size and scale of characters to backgrounds and props and to each other. Characters should be drawn correctly on model.

(3) Sketching Perspective

Storyboarding is a quick art. Therefore, we have to be able to quickly sketch not only people and cars but any object in perspective. The better you understand proper perspective, the more options you will have in designing your shots and making your sketches accurate and believable.

(4) Location

Locations should be researched or planned carefully before the board is started. Do floor plans, maps, rough blueprints, and so forth so you know your location well. The storyboard artist places doors, windows, furniture, and props in each room, and plans the placement of characters and the camera. The background should be simple so we can focus on the action.

(5) Composition

Next the storyboard artist considers what's the purpose of each scene? What is the visual focus? Keep reviewing your scenes to be sure that you're making your point clearly and that you don't lose it somewhere along the way. Which character is driving the action? Plan the action, reveal character, and discover the best composition for each shot. Be sure that the posing of your characters and the overall composition charge the scene with emotion. Make sure that there's enough room for the characters to move around and he can visualize the scene well. For really complicated action, the board artist may write out a shot list first. He emphasizes what's important in the story and downplays the rest, making only one point at a time. Simplicity is very important! The idea should be communicated instantly.

(6) Timing and Pacing

Pacing is important! Pace is varied throughout. Have you made good use of camera movement? Do your shots have a good rhythm to their sequence? Is each shot staged in the best way to tell the story? Shots normally get shorter, cuts faster as the climax nears. Dialogue is paced, unnecessary action skipped. A rhythm will be evident with the timing, but the board includes surprises to break the pace. Establishing shots are held long enough for the audience to take in the information. Audiences need time to absorb any important point. Audience emotions can be influenced by point of view, direction (left to right, or right to left), and composition. Does the action flow easily from one scene to another? Do you have good transitions between scenes? Clarity and continuity are very important.

(7) Characters

A good storyboard artist thinks like an animator, letting the characters act and show off their personalities. Mannerisms, body language, attitude/pose, stage business, and reaction shots all help define character. The faces on the characters reveal real emotions, not just blank stares. The storyboard poses are the best poses possible to reveal and show off each character. Characters in storyboards are posed in extremes. That means the poses are the most exaggerated poses in that scene with an imaginary and dynamic line. Each scene demands at least a start pose and an end pose. Any changes in action will normally be drawn as well. That way the layout artist will draw strong, exaggerated poses, giving animators and assistants strong action to animate.

Words and phrases

Close-Up   特写镜头
Medium Shot   中景镜头
Long Shot   远景镜头
Far Shot   全景镜头
Wide Shot   广角镜头，大全景
Upshot   仰视镜头
Downshot   俯视镜头
over the shoulder   过肩镜头
panoramic   平移，摇镜头
horizontally   水平地，地平地
track-in/track-out   镜头推进/镜头拉出
Zoom Shot   变焦镜头
fade in/ fade out   淡入/淡出
sweeping   彻底的，广泛的，弧线的
multiplane   多平面动画摄影
mundane   世俗的，平凡的
axis   轴，轴线
arrow   箭头
conjunction   结合，同时发生
foreground/ middle ground/ background   前景/中景/背景
rhythm   节奏，韵律
evident   明显的，明白的
clarity   清晰，明确

Practice

1. How to build a storyboard? Talk about the main workflow of it.

2. Create a storyboard for your story, if you don't have your own script, try storyboarding a novel or a sequence from one of your favorite films.

Translate into English

1. 优秀的故事板应包含各种各样的镜头，镜头长度也要有所变化，故事板画师通过调整摄像机来决定每个镜头的最佳角度，将所有想表达的东西展示给观众。

2. 一个好故事板画师的最重要的工作之一是创建镜头之间的平稳转场，所有镜头必须与前一个和后一个镜头很自然地衔接在一起。

Further reading

The Art of the Storyboard: A Filmmaker's Introduction
Editor: John Hart
Publisher: Focal Press (2007)

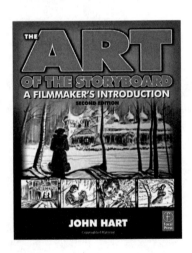

Web links

www.animatedstoryboards.com

Translation of text

摄像机镜头

优秀的故事板应包含各种各样的镜头，镜头长度也要有所变化。情节张力是通过情绪、气氛、画面构成和镜头变化来构建的。故事板画师通过变换摄像机角度呈现出不同的透视，以此来决定每个镜头的最佳角度，将所有想表达的东西展示给观众。摄像机角度是保持观众被故事吸引的一个关键因素，想象一下，如果整部片子你只看到一个视角会是什么感觉。

(1) 镜头角度
- 大特写：近到只能看见角色的眼睛、嘴、项链等。
- 特写：从肩膀到头部，用于要被注意的微妙面部表情或小细节。只是不要过度使用。
- 中景：拍摄到腰部，通常用在突显角色比周围环境重要的时候。可以展示面部表情和身体姿态。
- 中远景：拍摄角色膝盖以上的部分。
- 远景（定场镜头）：任何能拍到完整角色或远距离物品的镜头（包含背景）。
- 全景
- 大全景
- 广角镜头：给观众展示角色所在的位置。
- 仰视镜头
- 俯视镜头
- 过肩镜头：将焦点放在面对镜头的角色身上，但仍下意识地包含其他角色。

(2) 在故事板上的摄像机移动
- 平移、摇镜头：用摄像机水平移动来展示全景。如果在镜头平移过程中动作发生了变化，就要画出几个关键姿态。
- 镜头推进/镜头拉出：用摄像机在轨道上平滑的移动来捕捉场景里的动作。
- 变焦拍摄：用变焦镜头将焦点从全景转到特写。
- 摄像机调整：摄像机向任何方向的移动都小于一个完整的镜框。只显示结束点的完整镜框。

(3) 转场

一个好的故事板画师的最重要的工作之一是创建镜头之间的平稳转场。所有镜头必须与前一个和后一个镜头衔接在一起。不要总是直接切到下一个镜头，转场必须有创造性，要确保整个片子的流畅性，以及要很自然地进入到一个新的镜头。

在每个转场之前故事板画师都要写下以下几点之一：

- 淡入：摄像机的一种功能。打开光圈曝光从0%到100%需要几帧的时间。（开始是黑的，逐渐变亮）
- 淡出：摄像机的一种功能。关闭光圈曝光从100%到0%需要几帧的时间。（开始是亮的，逐渐变黑）
- 剪切：一个术语，用来描述当前场景的结束。下一个镜头与前一个镜头的地点或者角度均不相同，并与其是完全分开的。（场景的结束）
- 交叉溶解：淡入淡出的组合会产生一种"幽灵般"的效果，一个镜头消失的同时，另一个镜头出现。淡入和淡出的起始帧和结束帧是完全一致的。

像摄像机那样去思考

优秀的故事板画师会像摄像机那样去思考，考虑场景的拍摄角度，以及情节气氛是否需要摄像机移动。是否因为道具是一个重要的故事点而要给其一个特写？是否需要画出角色的反应？不要过度使用平移镜头或推拉镜头。当用平移或推拉镜头的时候，移动幅度要小。电脑动画的制片人通常鼓励弧线的摄像机移动。不论是传统动画还是电脑动画，以缓慢的推镜头与交叉溶解相结合使用会有多层次移动的感觉。

（1）用角度来讲述故事

以下几张图展示的是同一场景的不同拍摄角度。第一张图的背景画出了三个墙面，但是两个人的站位是挨着的，这样看起来很呆板没什么新意。第二张图就比较有活力。男青年离镜头比较近，这样就产生了深度。在镜头里他的位置比老人要高，所以这样看来男青年比较重要。在最后一张图里，男青年的位置几乎在画面最重要的位置。这样就非常有活力，但是要记住，只在适当的时候使用这种角度。

（2）水平线

仔细想想每一个镜头到底要讲述的是什么。适当地使用水平线可以增强镜头表现的力度。第一张图是一个很普通的镜头，看起来律师和法官的座椅所在的位置距离镜头是相等的。第二张图是一个比较有戏剧性的镜头。这张图与前一张几乎没有什么差别。但是，这次的焦点在法官身上，并且通过给他仰视镜头而加入了戏剧性元素。现在法官拥有更多的权力，并且强调了律师和他之间的距离。所有这些都要归功于降低了的水平线。

（3）仰视镜头和俯视镜头

大部分镜头都是直接平行拍摄的，仰视镜头和俯视镜头可以增加镜头变化和戏剧性。仰视镜头是将观众放置在焦点下方，而俯视镜头将观众放在焦点上方。

（4）屏幕方向：保持在摄像机轴线的同一侧

假想的摄像机从来不会以旋转超过 90 度的方式穿过假想的运动轴线。这样会迷惑观众。即使是两个人对话的特写，两个特写镜头的摄像机位置的交叉角也要小于 90 度。左图的摄像机位置是正确的。右图的摄像机架设在镜头来回切换的时候会让观众看不懂。故事板的绘制应该让摄像机保持在轴线的同一侧。

（5）屏幕方向：保持在屏幕的同一侧

通过在一组镜头里保持角色处在相同的相对空间里，来使剪切镜头干净利落。这有助于使你的表演和故事讲述保持清晰。

（6）屏幕方向：保持移动方向一致

我们阅读的时候视线习惯从左至右的移动，所以对眼睛而言从左至右比较自然。我们需要在汽车或角色行进方向的前方保留一定的空间，这样观众就会下意识地感觉他们有地方要去。

（7）插入镜头

应将全屏幕的动作、物件、文字或者角色反应的特写插入在一个较长的镜头里，或者插入在另一个角色的对白中间。当你选择镜头的时候，要在对观众的戏剧冲击力和视觉效果变化两方面作考虑。

练习

在加入草图之前，我们要把一组场景拆分成最基本的镜头。例如，一个男人正站在栅栏上，要展示整个人物和栅栏，这就叫远景。如果你想看这个男人在耳边举起了什么东西，就需要切到特写，原来他在耳边举起了一个小盒子。要画出一些箭头来表明这个男人正在来回摇晃这个盒子。接着我们切回到远景镜头，我们看到了一个女孩正在拉着一辆货车。如果我们从那个站在栅栏上的男人的视角想看货车里有什么，就会有个俯视的角度，一个蜘蛛侠的视角。我们可以将镜头切得近一些，看到在碗里有一条金鱼。镜头拉回到拉车女孩，她正在跟男人说话。从女孩的视角来看男人，是一个仰视的角度。这是一个壮观的镜头，就像看纪念碑或者巨人一样。当他将盒子递给女孩的时候，我们可以切换到侧景，这样我们就可以从侧面看到他们正在交换盒子。这使我们很想知道到盒子里到底有什么，想继续探索人物关系，想知道接下来会发生什么。

故事板

编写好影片的剧本后，接下来最重要的就是绘制故事板了。剧本以文字构成，故事板把剧本转为一系列摄像机视角的长方形图稿。它以比剧本更易让人理解的视觉方式来解释场景镜头以及整个故事板的内容。它更像是一本非常细致的漫画书。作为讲述故事的视觉工具，故事板可以让你很好地陈述自己的想法。

故事板将展示所有的镜头，向包括从动画制作人员到导演及制片人的所有人描述故事的情节发展。动画受到高额成本及冗长的制作过程的制约，所以所有的拍摄场景，一系列主要动作的图像化设计、摄像机位置、角度、镜头等细节必须在正式拍摄前决定好。

（1）故事板的格式

你可以自由地选择故事板的格式。故事板的基本概念是用图片和文字来叙述故事，包括导演的要求、音响效果及对白的说明。有些人喜欢标准的水平格式。有的人则偏好三栏式的故事板结构，其中的一栏用于附注和导演说明，一栏用于绘图，最后一栏用于对白。这是一种非常系统化的编写方式，可以和摄影表很好地结合在一起使用。无论你采用哪一种方法，都要使故事板中的每一个镜头或每一关键帧的图示风格更简练一点。你还可以在故事板中给摄像机的移动，如推、拉、摇、移，增加一些图形化的标注说明。

（2）绘制故事板

让我们开始将角色放置在一个个的长方形镜头框里来构建镜头。要绘制出一个好的故事板，要问自己以下几个问题：

- 这个故事讲述的是什么？
- 角色有哪些？他们要做什么，要说什么？
- 在前景、中景和背景里分别有哪些角色？
- 他们之间有冲突吗，与谁有冲突？
- 冲突发生在什么地方？
- 什么时候远景、中景和特写必须使用？

当绘制故事板草图的时候这些问题的答案就会变得清晰了。画师要先阅读剧本来熟悉情节和角色及其个性，然后要看模型表、可用的背景以及事先完成的动画草稿。他来决定角色与背景、道具之间以及角色与角色之间的大小和比例。角色应该按照模型准确地画出来。

（3）画出透视

绘制故事板需要快速地绘画。因此，我们不仅要快速地勾勒角色和汽车等的形象，还要画出他们的透视。透视理解得越透彻，你就会有越多的选择来设计你的镜头，可以使你的图稿又准确又可信。

（4）场景

场景在故事板开始绘制之前就应该仔细地作研究和规划。包括做平面布置图、地图、粗略的蓝图等，这样你就知道每一个场景的情况了。故事板画师在每一个房间里安排门、窗、家具和道具，设计角色和摄像机的位置。背景应该简单些，这样我们就能把注意力放在角色动作上。

（5）镜头组成

接下来故事板画师要考虑每一个镜头的目的是什么？视觉焦点是什么？反复地检查你的镜头以确保你的意图表达得很明确并且没有漏掉什么。哪一个角色是推动情节的？设计好动作情节，揭示角色性格，并且找出每个镜头的最佳组合。角色的姿态和整体构成使用情感元素来丰富镜头。确保给角色的移动留有足够的空间，这样画师就可以很好地设想镜头。对于非常复杂的情节，故事板画师会先写下镜头列表。他要强调什么是故事里最重要的，而对其他的就不那么重视，每次只有一个重点。保持简单是很重要的。想法应该被快速地传达出来。

（6）时间安排和节奏

节奏是非常重要的。节奏自始至终是变化的。你有没有很好地运用摄像机移动？你的一连串镜头有很好的节奏么？每一个镜头的表演是讲述故事的最佳方式么？在接近高潮的地方镜头通常越来越短，剪切得越来越快。对白是有节奏设定的，不必要的动作可以跳过。通过时间的安排节奏会变得清晰，但是故事板设定也包含打破节奏带来的意外效果。远景镜头通常会持续足够长的时间来使观众接受信息。观众需要时间来理解任何的关键点。观众的情绪会被镜头视角、方向（从左至右或从右至左）及画面组成所影响。情节是否很流畅地从一个镜头接另一个镜头？镜头之间有很好的转场过渡么？清晰度和连贯性是非常重要的。

（7）角色

一个好的故事板画师应该像动画师那样思考，让角色表演并且展示他们的个性。言谈举止、肢体语言、态度/姿势、表演以及反应镜头都会帮助塑造角色。角色的面孔揭示了真实的情感，而不仅仅是茫然困惑的眼神。故事板里的角色姿势可以揭示及展示每个角色最好的姿态。故事板里的角色被摆成最极端的姿势。这意味着这个姿势是镜头里的最夸张的姿势，是用想象力和充满活力的线条画出来的动作。每个镜头至少需要一个起始姿势和一个结束姿势。任何动作的改变也需要画出来。这样构图师就能画出表现力强、夸张的姿态，帮助动画师和助手来做动画。

4.5 Key, Extreme, Breakdown, and Inbetween
关键帧、原画、过渡位置和中间画

Text

In this chapter, we will learn the underlying principles and disciplines of animation technique. All animation can be broken down into definable stages. In general terms, these stages are key positions, extreme positions, breakdown or passing positions, and inbetween positions. Key positions are the storytelling drawings that show what's happening in the shot. The extreme positions are effectively the major positions in an action where that action ceases or changes direction in some way. The drawings in between the extremes were called the inbetweens.

Charts

Animators put charts on the edge of their drawings. The chart shows the extremes, inbetweens, and the different spacings on the drawing.

Now that you have the first chart drawn, let's talk about what it represents. Taking the numbers from the first extreme

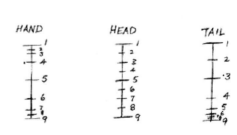

drawing (1) and the breakdown drawing (9), you will see the numbers 3, 5, and 7 evenly spaced between them. This shows the way that you need to draw the inbetweens. Similarly, the numbers from the breakdown drawing (9) to the second extreme drawing (17) are also equally spaced.

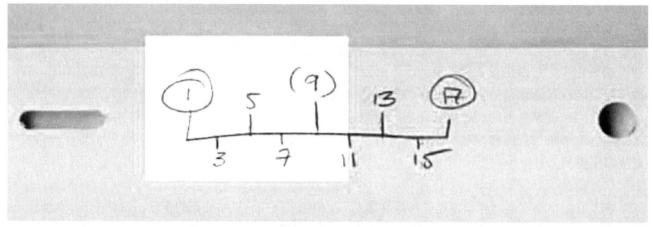

This clearly indicates that the drawings from 1 to 9 need to have even inbetweens.

Now let's get down to creating the inbetween drawings that are indicated on the chart. Number 5 is smack in the middle between 1 and 9. Then we put number 3 right in the middle between 1 and 5-and number 7 in the middle between 5 and 9. We've got the inbetweens spaced evenly.

Extremes, Breakdowns and Inbetweens

Take the example of a swinging pendulum: The extremes are where there is a change in direction.

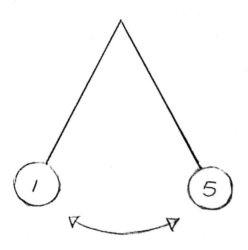

Because the pendulum's arm maintains its length as it swings, the middle position creates an arc in the action. It's so important to the action. We call this the "breakdown" drawing or "passing position" between two extremes.

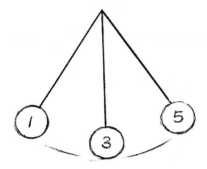
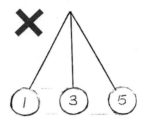

We'll add two in-betweens.

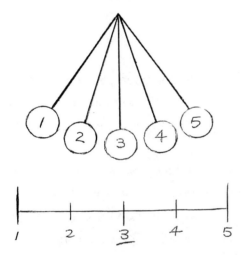

If we want to make our pendulum slow in and out of the extreme positions, we'll need a couple more inbetweens. So our chart will look like this.

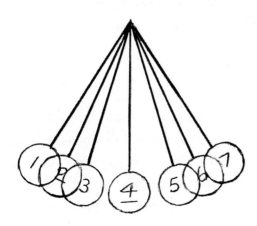
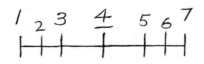

Keys

"Keys" are the storytelling drawings that show what's happening in the shot. These are the keys and we circle them. These are the drawings we make first. We don't circle any extreme positions, but the key drawing is. The drawings which are circled are the "Keys".

Take a more complex example: let's say a man walks over to a bookshelf, picks up a book from the floor and put it on the shelf.

If it was a comic strip or if we wanted to show what's happening on a storyboard, we'd need only three positions. These three positions become our keys and we circle them. All the other drawings or positions we'll have to make next to bring the thing to life will be the extremes (not circled): the foot "contacts", the passing positions or breakdowns and inbetweens.

If we time this action out with a stopwatch, we might find that our first key position at the start will be drawing 1. Say it takes him 2 seconds to walk over and contact the book on the floor-we'd circle the second key drawing as 48. And when he's stood up, picked up the book and put it on the shelf, it might take another 2 seconds-so our third key could be the last drawing in the shot -96. The whole shot would then take 4 seconds.

Many good animators call all their extremes "keys". But it's better to separate the storytelling keys from the extremes and all the other stuff. Separating them out stops us getting tangled up and missing the point of the shot, as we vanish into a myriad of drawings. There may be many keys in a scene-or maybe just one or two-it depends on what it is and the length of the scene. You can spend time on these keys.

The Best Way to Animate

First we decide what are the most important drawings, the storytelling drawings, the keys, and put them in. Then we put in any other important positions and poses that in the scene. These are the extremes, like anticipations or where hands or feet contact things. Now we have the structure. Now we use these keys and important extremes as guides for things and places we want to aim at. We may have to change and revise parts of the keys and extremes as we go along, rubbing bits off and redrawing or replacing them.

Then we work out how to go from one pose to another-finding the nicest transition between two poses. These are the breakdown or passing positions. Then we can make clear charts to cushion and slow in and out of the positions.

Let's take our man going over to the bookshelf again. First of all, I put in the keys-the storytelling drawings or positions that have to be there to show what's happening. Our first key position at the start will be drawing 1, second key drawing as 48, third key could be the last drawing in the shot -96.

Next, any other drawings have to be in the shot. Obviously, he has to take steps to get over to the book-so we make the "contact" positions on the steps where the feet are just touching the ground.

If we act all this out, we might find he takes two steps to get to the book and bend down. I notice that when I act it out, I automatically pull up my left pant leg as I bend down, then I put my hand on my knee before my other hand contacts the book. I would make an extreme where the hand just contacts the pant leg-before it pulls up the pants.

These will be my extremes. I'm working rough, sketching things in lightly, I'm trying to keep it simple, for clarity. We could act it out, timing the steps and putting numbers on the extremes, and test it on the video to see how the timing feels as his steps get shorter-and make any adjustments.

Next, we'll break it down, lightly sketching in our passing positions or "breakdowns". For now, we'll just make the head and body raise up slightly on the passing positions of the steps, like it does on a normal walk. When we test it, we've got three or four positions for every second, so it's easy to see what our timing is. It looks almost animated.

Now we'll make straight ahead runs on the different parts, using our extremes and breakdown positions as a guide-and altering them, or parts of them, if we need to as we go along. Take one thing at a time and animate it straight ahead.

To recap:

Having made the keys, put in the extremes, then put in the breakdowns or passing positions. Now that we've got our main thing-we go again, taking one thing at a time. First, the most important thing. Then, the secondary thing. Then, the third thing. Then, the fourth thing, etc. Then, add any flapping bits, drapery, hair, fat, breasts, tails etc.

The X-sheet

This is a "classic" exposure sheet called the X-sheet or dope sheet. It's just a simple and efficient form where animators write down the action and sound (or music beats) for a scene or shot-plus the information for shooting.

This "classic" X-sheet is designed to hold 4 seconds of action (1 second = 24 frames). Each horizontal line represents a frame of film. The columns 1 to 5 show five levels of animation we can use if we need them. The ACTION column is for us to plan out our timing-how long we want things to take. The SOUND column is for the measurement of the pre-recorded sound.

We'll plan out the action using the action column. We do the important part first-time it all out. So we'd use a metronome or a stopwatch and I'd act it out several times, and we'd mark down on the sheet where things would happen.

Let's take our man walking over to pick up the book. We've got him taking two steps to reach the book. When I act it out, the first step are leisurely-16 frames long (2/3 0f a second), during step 1 he sees the book. His second step is quickest-12 frames, on step 2 he's already started bending down, it takes over 14 frames till his hand contacts the book.

This becomes our guide and the points to aim for as we go along. Now we can put the numbers of these drawings on the page as I've done here. Incidentally, although numbers 1 and 96 are keys and we've circled them, we don't circle the numbers on the X-sheet.

The five levels on this X-sheet are there so we can treat each character or element separately. If we wish to use all five levels, start with the main action on level 1. Say a man walks in from one side of the screen and a cat walks in from the other. We animate our main action man on level 1, and the cat on level 2, adding a "C" after the cat numbers: 1-C, 2-C, 3-C etc., so as not to confuse it with the man drawing. The man drawings, or main action, don't need an identifying letter. If a woman passes in front of them, we'd put her on level 3, adding a "W" behind her numbers. If a truck was to stop in front of them, we'd use level 4 for the truck and add a "T" to the truck drawings. If it's raining, we'd put the rain drawings on level 5, adding an "R" after the numbers.

Pencil Tests

Pencil tests are quick samples of how the animation looks in motion. Constant testing of scenes helps the animator make timing and acting adjustments. Pencil tests are also used for approvals before the animation goes through clean-up and painting.

There are three ways to run a pencil test: you can use a hardware device without a computer, scan images into a computer, or capture images with a video camera into a computer. You also need Pencil test software programs for PC. So that, changing timings, adding frames, and deleting frames is simple. A big benefit to using a software pencil test system is that once your timings are set, you can print a dope sheet for reference.

Words and phrases

underlying 根本的
discipline 纪律，训练
comic strip 连环画，连载漫画
stopwatch 秒表
diagrammatic 图表的，图解的
tangle up 弄乱，缠在一起
myriad 无数的，种种的
recap 扼要重述
metronome 节拍器
scan 扫描

Practice

1. What are the advantages of the "pose to pose"?
2. What is an X-sheet? How to use X-sheet?

Translate into English

1. 动画师把运动标尺画在图画旁边，用来标明画中动作不同部分的空间幅度。
2. 最理想的动画方式就是先画出最重要的画，即故事板画和关键张，在此基础上画出其他重要的位置和动作，即原画，这样我们就有了结构。

Further reading

The Animator's Survival Kit
Editor: Richard E. Williams
Publisher: Faber and Faber (2009)

Web links

www.theanimatorssurvivalkit.com

Translation of text

在本小节中，我们将学习动画技术的基本原则和方法。所有的动画都可以分解成几个明确的步骤。一般而言，这些步骤是关键张位置、原画位置、小原画或过渡位置和中间画位置。关键张就是故事板画，也就是表示某一镜头内发生的故事的一张或多张画。原画实际上就是一个动作的几个主要位置，既一个动作以某种方式停止或改变方向的位置。在原画之间的画则被称为中间画。

运动标尺

动画师把运动标尺放在图画边上。标尺标明了画中动作不同部分的空间幅度。

现在已经画好了第一个运动标尺，让我们来说说它表示什么。你能看到3号、5号和7号在原画（1）与小原画（9）之间均匀地隔开。这就表明你需要在这些地方画出中间画。同样的，小原画（9）到第二个原画（17）之间的号码也要平均地间隔。

现在我们来画出运动标尺上表示的中间画。5号中间画挤在1号原画和9号小原画之间，然后我们把3号中间画放在1号原画和5号中间画之间，7号中间画放在5号中间画和9号小原画之间，这样中间画就被平均分布了。

原画、小原画和中间画

举个钟摆的例子：原画就是运动方向发生变化的地方。

由于钟摆摆动时，其臂长不变，所以中间的位置产生了弧线运动。这个中间位置的重要性显而易见。这个中间位置被称为两个原画之间的"小原画"或"过渡位置"。

下面我们再加上两个中间画。

如果想让钟摆在两个原画位置之间慢入慢出，那应该增加几个中间画。那么运动标尺应该是这样的。

关键张

"关键张"就是故事板画,即表示某一镜头内发生的故事的一张或多张画。这些就是关键张,我们把它们圈起来。这些就是我们要首先完成的部分。我们不圈任何一张原画,只圈关键张。所以圈起来的画就是"关键张"。

再举个复杂点儿的例子:一个人走到书架前,从地上捡起一本书然后放在书架上。

如果是画一本连环画或者我们想在故事板上表现这个过程,那么我们只需要这三张画就可以了。这三个位置就是关键张,我们把它们圈起来。后面画的其他所有的画或者位置都是为了让人物动起来,这些都是原画(没有被圈起来),比如脚"踩地"、过渡位置或小原画和中间画。

假如我们用秒表来计算这个动作的时间,会发现开始时的第一个关键位置要标示为 1 号。假如人物需要花 2 秒的时间走过,碰到地板上的书,我们把第二个关键位置标示为 48 号。接着,他起身走过,然后把书放到书架上,这要再花 2 秒的时间,所以我们把第三张关键画,也就是镜头的最后一张标示为 96 号。这样整个镜头会花上 4 秒的时间。

许多优秀的动画师把所有的原画看做是"关键张"。不过最好是把故事板关键张从原画和其他东西里分出来,这非常关键。分开是为了防止我们思绪混乱、抓不住镜头的关键,从而掉进无数张画的海洋中。一个场景中可能有很多关键张,也可能只有一两个,这取决于动作本身和场景的长度。你要花时间将这些关键张精雕细琢。

最理想的动画方式

首先我们决定哪些是最重要的画,即故事板画和关键张,先把它们放进来。然后放入其他重要的位置和动作,即原画,比如预备动作或手脚与物体的接触点。这样我们就有了结构。现在我们把这些关键张和重要的原画作为我们要画的物和场景的参考。随着工作的进程我们可能需要修改、添加、删除或重画某些关键张和原画。

然后再考虑如何从一个动作变到下一个动作,也就是要找到两个动作之间的最佳过渡。这个过渡就是小原画或过渡位置。这样我们就可以绘制一个清晰的标尺,游刃有余地加入缓冲、慢入和慢出。

再回到男人走向书架的例子。首先,我先放入关键张,即表现情节所必须的故事板图画或位置。开始的第一个关键张是 1 号,第二个关键张是 48 号,第三个关键张,也就是镜头的最后一张是96 号。

接下来,就是镜头所必须的其他所有的图画。不言而喻,这个人得一步一步去捡那本书,所以我们把接触位置放在双脚与地面接触的点上。

如果我们自己把这个动作表演出来,这个人可能要走 2 步才能拿到书并弯下腰。我注意到当我自己演示这个动作的时候,弯腰时无意识地拽起了左裤腿,一只手去拿书之前另一只手放在了膝盖上。我会在手拽起裤子之前画一张原画,也就是手刚刚接触裤腿的姿势。

这些画都会是我的原画。我轻轻地在这些图上画出草稿。我试图将草稿保持得简单、清晰。我们可以把这个动作实际演示出来,计算一下脚步,给原画标上号码,再录像测试,看看随着步伐变短,时间节点会产生什么变化,然后再作修改。

接下来,我们把动作分解开,轻轻地描出过渡位置或"小原画"。现在,只需要让头和身体在脚步的过渡位置上稍稍抬起来，就像正常走路时那样。我们测试的时候每一秒会得到 3 个或 4 个位置，这有助于判断我们的时间节点，并进行修改。现在这些画几乎就能产生动画的感觉了。

我们现在以原画和小原画为基础做出各部分的连续动作，如果需要，还可以在这个过程中对它们进行部分或整体修改。一次只做一个部分的逐张动画，这样循序渐进。

练上所述，我们画了关键张，也做了原画，也加上了小原画或过渡位置。这样我们就搭起了一个骨架，然后每次都按照这个顺序完成每一件事。首先，画最重要的图；然后，画第二重要的图；接着，画第三重要的图；随后，再画第四重要的图……最后加上飘动的部位、服饰、头发、肥肉、胸膛、尾巴等。

摄影表

这是一张"经典"的摄影表，也叫做律表。它只是一张动画师用来记录一个场景或镜头内的动作和对白（或音乐节拍），再加上摄影要求的简单有效的图表。

这张"经典"的摄影表用来表示 4 秒的动作（1 秒 =24 格）。每条水平的线表示影片的一格。1~5 栏表示我们可能需要用到 5 个动画层次。动作栏用于安排时间节点，即做一个动作需要的时间。对白栏用于测算先期录音的对话。

我们用动作栏来设计一个动作。先把重要的部分做出来，算好动作的时间。我将把一个动作做几次，然后我们用节拍器或秒表进行测试，顺着摄影表标出动作发生的位置。

再回到人走过来捡书的例子。我们让这个人走两步来到书前。我自己做这个动作时，第一步比较轻松，用了 16 格（即 2/3 秒），在第一步的时候他已经看到了那本书。走第二步时速度稍微加快，用了 12 格。在第二步时他已经开始弯腰，用了 14 格接触到那本书。

这就是我们往下进行工作时的参照点。现在我们可以把各图的号码记在表上。虽然在此 1 号和 96 号图是关键张——通常我们会把它们圈起来，但在摄影表上，我们不把关键张的号码圈起来。

摄影表上已经存在 5 个动面分层，这样我们就可以利用它们分别处理每个角色或元素。如果 5 个分层我们都想使用，那么主要动作应该先用"层 1"。比如，一个人从屏幕一侧入画，一只猫从另一侧入画，那么我们用"层 1"表示这个人的主要动作，用"层 2"表示猫的主要动作，在猫的动作号码后加一个字母 C，如 1-C，2-C，3-C，等等，这样就不会与人的动作编号混淆，人的主要动作图则不需要添加识别字母。如果一个女人从他们面前经过，我们会用"层 3"表示她的动作，在她的动作号码后面加一个字母"W"。如果一辆卡车在他们面前停下，我们会用"层 4"表示卡车的动作，在它的动作号码后面加一个字母"T"。如果下着雨，我们就用"层 5"表示，在下雨的动作号码后面加一个字母"R"。

铅笔稿测试

铅笔稿测试是用来快速浏览动画效果的。反复做稿测试可以帮助动画师对时间和动作作调整。铅笔稿测试也用于批准动画可以进入到清稿和上色阶段。

有三种方式可以来进行铅笔测试：你可以使用一个硬件设备，无需电脑，将图像扫描到电脑里，或用摄像机捕捉图像到电脑里。你还需要针对电脑的铅笔稿测试软件。这样，改变时间、添加帧和删除帧都会很简单。使用铅笔稿测试系统的一个很大的好处是，一旦时间设置确定好了，就可以打印摄影表以供参考。

4.6 Background Layouts and Paint
背景构图与上色

Text

The next things that need to be attended to before your produce your animation are backgrounds and layouts. Once the layout artists receive the storyboard, prop, location and character designs, with character movement in mind, the work begins. The focus of the layout artist is to dissect the storyboard scene by scene, and looking for: perspective, required camera shots and angles, composition and staging, and element placement. The layout artists dictate the quality and direction the artwork will take on.

Layouts

Layouts are the drawings of the backgrounds that the background painter will use. Using the storyboards or production illustrations as a base, we design the layouts to work with the action, so that the layout works with the flow of the story.

In the layout phase the look of a scene is finalized, and each shot is made as dynamic and as helpful to the story as possible. Each shot should be composed with great skill and care, with the aim of focusing the audience on what the director has specified and creating the greatest visual impact possible. Each shot also needs to properly follow the visual cues from the previous scene and lead into the following scene.

Other visual layout issues to pay attention to are balance, negative space, motion, straight on shots, angled shots, and all the other rules of proper and exciting composition. Visually, the audience's eye should be guided to the most important point in the shot, such as the lead character or a crucial prop. Once a layout is approved, the animators may use it to animate over. Animators only need a black and white line version of any background—in fact. While the animators are working, the background painters will fill in and enhance the layout.

The layouts are given to the animators and the background artists. The animators plan their characters' positions based on the layouts. If any portion of the background image changes position during the painting process, it may completely disrupt what the character does in the scene; in addition, a character may no longer line up with the background.

However, before describing the actual process of creating layouts, we should first look at some of the rules of layout design that will affect their creation. The following are just a few pointers that apply to pretty much all visual art imagery. But they are particularly pertinent to creating background and layout design in animation.

Background Layout Elements

(1) Distance and Perspective

Perspective is a theory of drawing, which allows the artist a way to graphically depict three-dimensional objects on paper or other media, as they exist in space.

(2) Horizon Line (HL)

Horizon line is the continuous distant line at which the eye can see no further. Depending on what angle you look up or down, the horizon line position changes and is not always visible.

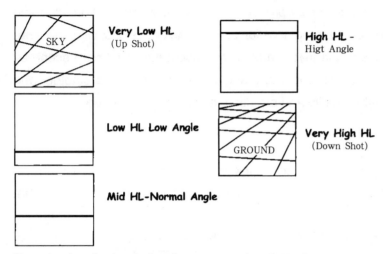

Five examples of various horizon lines.

(3) Eye Level

The level at which you are standing and looking at an object is known as the eye level. Eye level and the horizon line are tied directly together.

(4) Point of View (P.O.V.)

Can be described as what you see from where you are looking.

(5) Station Point

This is the point from which the audience is looking from.

(6) One Point (Parallel) Perspective

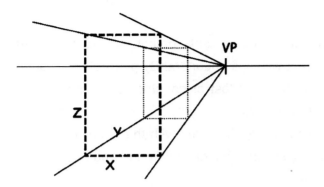

(7) Two Point (Angular) Perspective

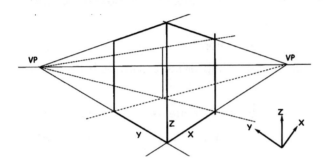

(8) Three Point (Oblique) Perspective

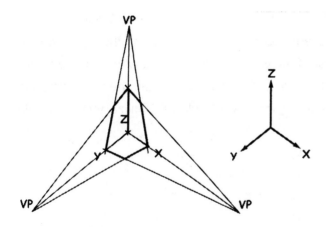

The layout artist should remember that these levels of distance and perspective will bring a great vision and depth to a shot, whether an internal environment or external landscape. In other words, many of the most powerful and attractive scenes contain a clear foreground, midground, and distant view.

(9) Focus of Attention

Most scenes require that the animation be the focus of attention. Therefore, when you work on your background layouts, make sure the area that the animation is to appear in is uncluttered, use lines and objects converge on the point where you want the main action to be seen. This is most easily achieved with perspective lines, but not always. Not doing so will clearly diminish the impact of your character's effectiveness within the scene.

(10) Element Placement

As the responsibilities of the layout artist, the composition, element placement, the creation of an atmosphere that a character could freely move and interact within is important. By placing background elements in various positions the character in front can become lost or constricted for movement. Similar problems occur when placing elements in front of the character.

Foreground: An element that is up close and usually partially illustrated with the remainder of the object situated off the page. The foreground is used in conjunction with the midground and background areas of an environment.

Midground: In conjunction with the foreground and background areas of an environment, the midground is the main acting stage for the animation to take place. Objects in this area should not interfere the animation.

Background (BG) or Distant: The background is the furthest portion of the environment, such as mountains, trees, clouds or stars in space. Generally there is very little detail drawn with the distant element.

By combining the foreground, midground and distant levels, a strong visual is created. Using these elements and perspective together creates depth. How the elements are arranged is just as important as what is arranged within a scene.

Process

Now we can turn to the actual process of creating layouts. These layouts are separated into two types: those that define things that don't move in the scene (background layouts) and those that define things that will move (animation layouts). However, first of all, you should establish what field size your film is going to be animated within — that is, 10 field, 12 field, or 16 field. On a fresh sheet of animation paper, draw the boundaries of your chosen field size using thick black ink, and utilize this as a field guide for all your subsequent layout drawings.

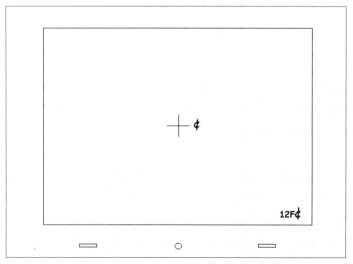

A12 field-size layout guide with the screen center position marked.

Then, with a fresh sheet of paper laid over the top of the field guide, rough out your first thoughts for the shot, based on the storyboard frame you've already created. If you have a clear and detailed storyboard drawing for the scene, you might even copy or enlarge your storyboard frame to the final layout size and tape it onto the animation paper to become your rough layout.

Next, you might ask yourself:
- Is this rough layout giving me the depth, dimension, drama, and dynamics I am looking for in the scene?
- Does this layout showcase the necessary animation in the best way possible?
- Did I get the perspective and scale right?
- Is the character in correct proportion and position to everything else?

When you have asked yourself these questions, you will want to work more on what you have, until you are really satisfied. Eventually you will come up with your final rough layout and that will be the time to move on to the next stage.

(1) Dividing the Layout

With the final rough layout to guide you, begin separating the two elements: the background and animation layouts.

For the background layout, place a new sheet of paper over your rough layout and begin to accurately draw everything in the scene that does not move. For purposes that will become apparent later, make sure your layout drawing line is dark and strong.

However, if you have a foreground element in the scenes that need to go in front of the animation, you should draw all those foreground elements onto a separate sheet of paper, so that the entire scene is made up of three levels: the background, character, and foreground.

Next, you need to focus on the animation layout or layouts. You'll need to draw more than one animation layout design for your character. Usually within any particular scene storyline there is a beginning, middle, and end to the action. Therefore, these animation layout drawings will appear on separate layers.

(2) Paint Backgrounds

Backgrounds may be completed in any number of styles using any number of tools. Many animators and studios use Photoshop or Painter for their backgrounds. Others may prefer actual paint, pastels, pencils, photos, or even CG backgrounds.

The backgrounds should be designed to enhance the flow of a project. Make sure that the look and color of the backgrounds work together in each scene. Keep the same tonal values and color in all the backgrounds of that sequence. Another important color issue to watch for is ensuring that your characters stand out. It is not a good idea to have a background that is the same color as your character's clothes.

When backgrounds are painted in a computer program, the layout drawings are usually finished by hand, scanned at a higher resolution than we needed so that we would have room to push in, zoom in, on a scene if we wanted. We import each layout into Painter or Photoshop, background painter paint depending on the paint effects they need. It's a good idea to paint different sections and objects on separate layers. For instance, the ground may be on layer 1, the foreground trees on layer 2, and the sky on layer 3.

We save our backgrounds with layers as Adobe Photoshop files. When we import the files into Adobe After Effects for compositing, we can use the layers to allow our animated characters to easily pass behind foreground objects. The separate layers also provides us with more opportunities for utilizing effects such as glows, shadows, and color shifts during compositing.

When a scene needs a background to pan, the size of the layout must be large enough to accommodate the camera move. However, if the pan is so long that the background needs to be cycled, that should be laid out at least 2 fields wide, or twice the width of the frame.

Words and phrases

dissect 仔细分析，剖析，分成小块
disrupt 破坏，使中断
pertinent 相关的，中肯的，切题的
horizon line 地平线，水平线
converge 汇聚，集中于一点
effectiveness 效果，有效性
interfere 干扰，干涉
utilize 利用，运用
pastel 色粉笔
resolution 分辨率
accommodate 容纳，适应，调节

Practice

1. Try to explain the whole process of background layouts and paint.
2. What is the key point to make the best layouts for an animated film?

Translate into English

1. 透视是绘画的一种基本理论，根据这个理论艺术家可以绘制出逼真的三维效果的物体。
2. 每个镜头都应该以高超的技巧和谨慎的态度来设计，目的就是尽可能地将观众的注意力集中在导演营造出的视觉冲击力上。

Further reading

Walt Disney Animation Studios-the Archive Series: Layout & Background
Editor: John Lasseter
Publisher: Disney Editions (2011)

第 4 单元　制作动画电影　129

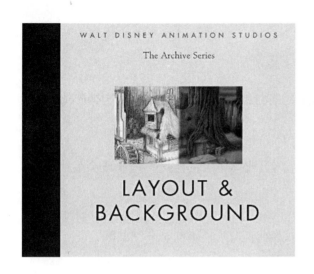

Web links

www.animationbrain.com

Translation of text

在做动画之前需要明确的事情是背景和构图。一旦构图画师收到故事板、道具、场景和角色设计，对角色动作有了构思之后，就开始做构图设计了。构图画师要关注的重点是对一个接一个的场景进行仔细的分析，并且要寻找：透视、必要的摄像机拍摄角度、画面构成和布局，以及各个元素的位置。构图画师对作品的质量和方向有着决定性的影响。

构图设计

构图就是背景设计的图稿，这些是背景画师将要用到的。以片子的故事板和概念设计为基础，我们设计出构图来配合角色动作，这样构图才能更好地有助于故事的讲述。

在构图阶段场景设计应该是已经完成的，而且每一个镜头被设计得尽可能地有活力，尽可能地对故事有所帮助。每个镜头都应该以高超的技巧和谨慎的态度来设计，目的就是尽可能地将观众的注意力集中在导演营造出的视觉冲击力上。每个镜头也需要恰当地遵循前一个镜头的视觉线索，同时也要引入到下一个镜头中去。

构图要注意的其他问题是画面平衡、负空间、运动、直接拍摄、有角度的拍摄，以及其他所有合理的和有意思的构图规则。从视觉上来看，观众的眼睛应该被镜头里最重要的点所引导，比如主要角色或者一个重要道具。构图通过后，动画师可以用它来呈现动画。实际上，动画师只需要背景的黑白稿就可以了。动画师在制作动画的同时，背景画师将给背景上色来加强画面构图。

构图绘制好了之后就交给动画师和背景画师。动画师根据构图来安排角色的位置。如果在绘制过程中背景图像的位置发生变化，则会完全打乱场景里的角色动作；此外，角色和背景也将无法对位。

在讲解构图设计的具体制作过程之前，我们应该先来了解一些构图设计的规则，这些将会影响创作的结果。以下几点规则适用于所有的视觉艺术图像设计，但是它们对动画里的背景和构图创作特别有用。

背景布局元素

（1）距离和透视

透视是绘画的一种基本理论，根据这个理论艺术家可以在纸上或其他介质上绘制出物体逼真的三维效果，就像它们存在于空间中一样。

（2）地平线

地平线是眼睛能看到的无限遥远地方的延伸线。根据你向上或向下看的角度，地平线会发生变化，并且不总是可见的。

（3）视平线

你所站的并看向一个物体的水平位置叫做视平线。视平线和地平线是紧密联系在一起的。

（4）焦点

焦点可以解释成从你观察的位置所能看到的东西。

（5）视点

观众视线的出发点。

（6）一点透视

（7）两点透视

（8）三点透视

构图画师应该记住这些距离和透视将会给镜头带来很好的视觉效果和深度，不论是室内环境还是室外场景。换句话说，很多非常有冲击力和吸引力的镜头都包含清晰的前景、中景和远景。

（9）关注的焦点

大多数镜头要求动画是画面的焦点。因此，当你设计背景构图的时候，要确保动画出现的区域是整洁的，用线条或者物体将观众视线汇聚到你想要表现的主要动作。用透视线就可以很容易达到这个目的，但不是每次都这样。如果不这样做就会降低场景中角色的感受力。

（10）元素的放置

作为构图画师的责任，画面构成、元素的位置、角色可以自由移动及相互作用的气氛营造，这些都是非常重要的。背景元素不同位置的摆放会使前景的角色被挡住或者活动受到限制。类似的问题在摆放角色前层的元素时也会发生。

前景：是离镜头最近的元素，并且通常会将位于画面之外的物体的一部分画出来。前景用来连同场景的中景、背景区域一起使用。

中景：用来连同场景的前景和背景一起使用，中景是动画表演的主要区域。这个区域的物体应该不要干扰到动画。

背景或者远景：背景是场景里最远的部分，像远山、树、云彩或者天空里的星星。通常对远景元素不需要画出什么细节。

将前景、中景、远景相组合后，很好的视觉效果就会出现了。将这些元素及透视结合使用就会使画面产生纵深感。如何布置这些元素就如同布置一个场景里所有的东西一样重要。

设计步骤

现在我们开始进入到构图设计的具体创作步骤。我们把构图分成两种类型：一类是在场景里不需要移动的元素（背景构图），另一类是需要移动的元素（动画构图）。但是，首先我们应该确定画面的规格，即 10 号、12 号或 16 号规格。在一张空白的动画定位纸上，我们把画面规格的边线描成粗黑的，把这个框子作为后续构图设计的规格框。

然后，再取一张定位纸叠放在规格框上面，根据已有的分镜头画稿画出镜头构思的草稿。如果你有非常清晰明确的分镜头画面，你只需要把分镜头画稿复制或者放大成最终构图的尺寸并粘贴到动画纸上，就可以将其作为构图草稿使用了。

接下来，你需要问自己几个问题：
- 这个构图草稿有没有表现出镜头的纵深感、立体感、戏剧效果和动感？
- 这种构图是否是展示动画的最佳方式？
- 画面透视和比例缩放都正确么？
- 角色的比例和位置对整个画面来说是否正确？

当你问过自己这些问题后，你就会知道如何来修改画面构图了，直到你自己真的满意为止。最后，你的构图草稿完成后，就可以进入到下一个阶段。

（1）划分构图

参照最后的构图草稿，你可以将画面元素分成两类：背景构图和动画构图。

对于背景构图，在构图草稿上叠放一张空白纸，开始精确地描画出场景里所有不会动的东西。为了之后效果会明显些，要确保你的构图线条画得很黑很重。

但是，如果场景里有前景并且会遮挡住动画，你应该将所有的前景元素画在单独的一张纸上，这样整个场景就会被分成三层：背景、角色和前景。

接下来，你需要把重点放在动画构图上。你需要给角色绘制出多个构图设计。通常在任何一个特定的场景情节里，角色动作都会有一个开始、中间及结束。因此，这些动画构图要分层来画。

（2）背景绘制

背景可以用不同的工具画成不同的风格。很多动画工作室使用 Photoshop 或 Painter 这两款软件来绘制背景。其他的则喜欢用真实的绘画、蜡笔、铅笔、照片或者电脑制作的背景。

背景的设计应该能够提升片子的质量。要确保每个场景的设计和色彩能够配合得很好。要保持一组镜头里所有背景的色调一致。另一项重要的用色事项是要能够突出角色。背景不能和角色衣服使用相同的颜色。

用电脑软件绘制背景的时候，构图是手绘完成的，然后扫描成高分辨率的图片，这样在需要的时候我们就有空间来推近镜头和放大场景。

我们把每张构图导入到 Painter 或 Photoshop 里，背景画师用各种需要的绘制效果来绘制背景。将背景不同的部分和对象分层来绘制是个好方法。比如，地面在层 1，前景的树在层 2，天空在层 3。

我们将分层绘制的背景保存成 Photoshop 文件。当我们将文件导入到 Adobe After Effects 里做合成的时候，我们就可以使角色动画很容易地在前景物体后面穿过。分层文件也给我们提供了更多的利用特效的机会，比如发光、阴影及在合成过程当中的颜色变化。

当一个镜头需要背景平移的时候，构图的尺寸必须足够大以容纳摄像机的移动。但是，如果平移的距离太长，则背景需要做成循环的，那背景就应该展开成至少两倍场景的宽度，或者两倍镜头规格的宽度。

4.7 Post-Production

后期制作

Text

Rendering

Rendering is the stage in production when all the data generated during the digital process, are brought together and converted into a film file that can be played on a standard digital movie player. The file formats most conventionally used are mov (QuickTime), avi (Windows Media), MP4 (Website, Smart phone).

Before you even start animating you really need to consider the size of the screen format you want to use, the quality of image you need to render, and the speed of frames per second (fps).

(1) Screen Format Ratio

The screen format ratio really has to be decided first, before you even begin to put pencil to paper. For example, a 4 : 3 ratio is for a standard TV or computer monitor, a widescreen format ratio is for cinematic projection and HD TV.

(2) Resolution

Most TV and computer monitors use a 72-ppi resolution. Consequently, for academy format images on most monitors or screens, we are looking at a full-screen image measurement of 720 × 480 pixels (or 720 × 576 pixels for TV and other PAL-based regions). HD screens, however, require a larger screen dimension. One of the most standard is 1920 × 1080 pixels.

(3) Frame Rates

When animating and rendering your film, you should also become aware of the fps projection rate. The standard projection rate for film is 24 fps. TV projection rate is 30 fps (NTSC broadcast regions), 25 fps (PAL broadcast regions). Consequently, it is essential to know the correct frame rate for your project before you start to draw or create your animation, as well as when you render your final movie footage.

You do not have to wait until the very end of your production to render all your final scenes. It is invariably normal practice to render each scene as you finish it and safely store them all for when you complete your entire final render and edit.

Editing

Since most animation is digitally painted and composited, you will most likely use a digital nonlinear editing program. Programs such as Adobe Premiere, is a popular nonlinear editing tool that works very well on PCs. (Mac users could use Final Cut Pro.) During editing, you will compile all of your production elements, title cards, credits, footage, sound effects, music, dialogue, and more.

To edit a film, first, upload the separate scene files into the bin provided, then drag them in the correct order into the timeline. Next, import audio tracks, especially the sound effects tracks, which you will line up with the picture by trial-and-error sliding to ensure that everything is in sync. With everything lined up and synchronized, review your film by clicking the "Play" icon to see it run in the preview screen.

You may find that you need to lengthen or shorten a cycled sequence to make a scene feel right. Maybe a title card needs to be held longer. The length of a single frame sometimes makes a big difference, so remove and add single frames until it felt just right.

You may also find that you need to rearrange the order of your scenes to have the story make more sense, or to heighten the drama. Be open to rearranging scenes if necessary. Working with nonlinear editing systems makes this very easy and fast.

The final audio needs to be timed to the final video length. Then you will take the finished audio file, most likely in .wav or .aif format, and drop it into your nonlinear editing program for final output. When you edit the sound in your edit program, you will use many levels of overlapping audio for the dialogue, effects, and music. As you layer in your audio files, you will need to balance the levels of each so the dialogue is easy to understand and none of the audio is distorted.

You always hope that your animation is perfectly synced to the audio, but dialogue often has to be rerecorded. Take great care to match the sync of the new audio to the animation; it will be worth your time.

In most animation, you will not need to worry about adjusting the color levels of your scenes. However, if you are mixing any stop-motion footage, you may find that you need color adjustment. Color shifts in video footage happen most often when the camera was not properly balanced to white for each scene.

Editing programs offer filmmakers many different styles of transitions. The best transitions to use are simple cuts and dissolves. Watch your favorite films and TV shows and you will notice only cuts and dissolves.

Once your edit is complete, make sure to back up your files, if all is well, it's time do a quick, small-size render.

Music and Sound Design

(1) Music

With all the visuals in place and looking good, you should consider the music content, as well as make a note of the points where you'll need sound effects to support the action. Music and sound effects are the final touches that give your project life. The right music can help your animation flow, and sound effects can give your work a solid feeling that adds to the illusion of life.

You should have a professional music and sound design company or studio to produce music; they will need the final edit of your animation to work with. They provide you with a few samples of music based on the style of music you asked for, and add all the sound effects, then produce a custom music track that support the action in your film. Once their work was done, they provided you with a stereo .wav file that you could drop into your Premiere edit suite.

(2) Sound Effects

In addition to music, you will also probably need to add sound effects to your film to lift the quality of its audio content. For example, if a character is running on a muddy surface, you will probably need to hear that surface squelch every time the character's foot hits it.

There are two ways of acquiring sound effects for your audio track: getting them ready-made from sound effects libraries or recording them yourself. Online sound effects libraries, such as www.sounddogs.com, www.sound-ideas.com, www.soundfx.com have a vast supply of sounds that you can listen to online and acquire. If you need sound effects that are entirely original and unique to your film, you will have to work harder to obtain them. Most sounds can be created live. For example, if you want a busy-street sound, it is very easy to point a microphone toward your local main road and record the sounds direct.

In Premiere we placed the music on one level and added the audio on a number of other levels. We then go through the entire project and adjust the audio levels. Once the audio is complete, we are ready to output the file to tape or to film.

Final Composite

You've finished your project. With animation placed and colored on different layers, the background on the bottom layer, and a title or even animated effects on a top layer, the music is perfect, and all the sound effects are in. Do your final composite to check every frame, render the whole thing out into a movie format. If there's a problem with one frame, don't worry about it, which only happens a few times on every project. You should go back, re-export that frame, re-export the affected scene, and built a new file in your edit suite. Here, I would like to just mention a few key compositing approaches you might want to consider.

(1) Layers

Often it is necessary to combine separate layers of action to create a specific effect. To achieve various specific parallax-layered effects, you should use Adobe After Effects, although other programs such as Autodesk's Combustion work equally well. After Effects is something of a mix between Adobe Photoshop and Adobe Premiere. As with Photoshop, After Effects enabled us to remove matted areas of each layer that we don't want the audience to see via alpha channels.

(2) Transparency

Another possibility of compositing your work in separate layers is the fact that you can create things like a transparent visual effect. This is essentially something that is easy to create, whether the object of attention is moving or static. However, if you don't have After Effects or a program like it, you can achieve the same effect in something like Adobe Photoshop, then composite everything in a film-editing program like Adobe Premiere.

(3) Cycle Animation

If you want to show character walk from the far right of the screen to the far left, use a repeat walk cycle with a long-panning background action, and a tree overlay. This is something that digital technology is especially good at. As scenes are created in layers, it is possible to place the walk action on the upper layer and pan the background artwork past it on the lower layer. This gives the very effective illusion of the camera is tracking along a scene with the character.

(4) Depth of Field

Lastly, the ultimate sense of depth in a scene can be achieved by manipulating its depth of field. This effectively means changing its focus throughout its various layers. Throw the background out of focus while keeping the foreground action sharp, the opposite is effective too, with the foreground blurred and the background sharp.

(5) Titles and Effects

Most projects have or need an opening sequence showing the title of the project. These title sequences can be either static or moving, even animated, they can be anything you desire, and you should try to have them work with or enhance the theme of the production.

Most of the title cards are produced in Adobe Photoshop. The files are made to be the same size of your video files, but since NTSC pixels are rectangular and Photoshop pixels are square, you need to adjust for the different shaped pixels in the size of your images. The animated title sequences are built in After Effects.

Once your design is complete, you should export the image to any RGB file type that your compositing or editing program can work with. We usually export either .tga or .tif files, which are uncompressed.

All important imagery and text needs to be within the safe areas or safe zones. Every television cuts off a different amount of the entire image that is projected. Title safe is the area of the frame where all text should be kept, and action safe represents the boundaries for any important graphic or motion. Compositing and editing programs allow you to view these boundaries as you work.

The timing of your title cards is also important. You need to make sure that the average viewer has enough time to read everything on the screen, and doesn't get tired of it. Practice will help you determine what is the appropriate length of time to have any cards on the screen.

(6) Credits

There are three basic ways to produce your credits: ① they can be single graphic cards; ② they can be produced within your edit suite; ③ they can be built in a compositing program. If your show has only a few names that you need to credit, you can make some graphics cards and either set the timing in your editing program or in your compositing program. Otherwise, you will most likely want a rolling credit list. If you find that the effects don't work in quite the same way that you envisaged, research other techniques and approaches that might work better for you.

Words and phrases

fps(frames per second)　每秒帧数，帧率
screen format ratio　屏幕格式比
widescreen　宽屏，大银幕
cinematic projection　电影投影
HD TV　高清电视
pixel　像素，像素点
PAL　一种电视广播制式，每秒25帧，电视扫描线为625线，奇场在前、偶场在后，电视标准分辨率为720×576，24比特的色彩位深，画面的宽高比为4：3，主要应用于中国、欧洲等国家和地区。
NTSC　一种电视广播制式，每秒29.97帧（简化为30帧），电视扫描线为525线，偶场在前、奇场在后，电视标准分辨率为720×486，24比特的色彩位深，画面的宽高比为4：3，主要应用于日本、美国、加拿大、墨西哥等国家和地区。
compile　编译，编制，编辑
trial-and-error　试错法，反复试验法，尝试法
sync　同步
stereo　立体声
squelch　噪声控制
alpha channel　透明通道
rectangular　矩形的，长方形的
square　正方形
RGB(red, green, blue)　红、绿、蓝颜色表示法
uncompressed　未压缩的，无压缩的
envisage　设想，想象

Practice

1. Watch some short films, animated or otherwise, to see how scenes are cut together.
2. Talk about the workflow of post-production.

Translate into English

1. 由于大多数动画是用电脑绘制及合成的，所以在后期制作的时候你将很可能用到一个数字非线性编辑软件。

2. 要剪辑一部电影，首先要将所有的镜头片段导入到剪辑软件里，然后将它们按照正确的顺序拖拽到时间线上。

Further reading

Designing Sound for Animation
Editor: Robin Beauchamp
Publisher: Focal Press (2005)

Web links

www.designingsound.tv

Translation of text

渲染

渲染就是在数字化制作过程中将所有数据最终生成出来的阶段，在这个阶段中所有数据将被整合到一起并转化成能用标准播放器播放的影片文件。文件格式最常用的是 mov(QuickTime)、avi(Windows Media) 和 mp4（网站、智能手机）。

在你开始制作动画之前，你需要考虑屏幕格式的大小、需要渲染的图像质量以及帧率（每秒多少帧）。

（1）屏幕格式比例

屏幕格式比例是需要最先考虑的事情，在你起笔绘制草稿之前就要确定下来。比如，4∶3 的比例是针对标准电视机和电脑显示器的，宽屏格式比例是针对电影放映和高清电视的。

（2）分辨率

大多数电视和电脑显示器使用 72ppi 的分辨率。因此，标准格式的图片在显示器或屏幕上是全屏显示的，大小为 720×480 像素（或为 720×576 像素，针对电视及其他 PAL 制地区）。但是，高清的屏幕则需要更大的尺寸。最标准的格式之一是 1920×1080 像素。

（3）帧率

当制作动画或者渲染影片的时候，你应该要注意帧率。电影播放的标准帧率是 24 帧/秒。电视播放的帧率是 30 帧/秒（使用 NTSC 制的地区），及 25 帧/秒（使用 PAL 制的地区）。因此，在你开始起笔绘制或者做动画之前，以及当你渲染最终影片的时候，知道片子的正确帧率是非常关键的。

你不必等到整个片子的内容都完成的时候才开始渲染所有的最终场景。在实际工作中，通常是每一个镜头完成后就开始渲染，并且要把数据都保存好以备最终渲染和剪辑的时候使用。

剪辑

由于大多数动画是数字化绘制和合成的，你将很可能用到一个数字非线性编辑软件。比如 Adobe Premiere 就是一个在 PC 平台上非常流行的非线性编辑工具（苹果电脑用户可以使用 Final Cut Pro）。在剪辑过程中，你要将片子所有的素材汇总，包括标题卡、演职员名单、镜头片段、音响效果、音乐、对白，等等。

要剪辑一部电影，首先要将所有的镜头片段导入到剪辑软件里，然后将它们按照正确的顺序拖拽到时间线上。接着导入音轨，尤其是音响效果，你要通过反复地滑动来将音响效果与画面对位，以确保所有音画都是同步的。所有内容都对准并同步后，点击"播放"按钮在预览屏幕内来检查影片的运行情况。

你可能会发现你需要加长或者缩短某个循环序列使镜头感觉更好。或许一个标题卡需要延长时间。某一帧时长的改变有时候会使效果大有不同，所以你可以反复地移除或是添加单帧直到效果满意为止。

你也可能会发现你需要重新排列镜头的顺序来使故事更有意思或增强戏剧性。所以要尽可能地调整镜头顺序。用非线性编辑系统可以很容易并很快速地完成这些。

最终的音频需要根据最终的视频长度来设定时间。然后你将完成的 wav 或 aif 格式的音频文件导入到非线性剪辑软件里做最终的输出。当你在剪辑软件里编辑声音的时候，你将会用到很多叠加的音频层来处理对白、音响效果及音乐。当你分层处理音频文件时，你需要平衡每个层的音量级别，这样对白就能很容易地被听到，并且所有的音频效果都不会失真。

你总是希望你的动画片完全是音画同步的，但是对白通常要不停地反复录制。对新的音频与动画的同步对位要特别小心仔细，这是值得花费时间来做的。

在制作大多数动画片的时候，你无需担心校正画面的颜色。但是，如果你处理某些定格动画片段时，你就会发现你需要做色彩校正。视频片段里的颜色发生变化经常是因为摄像机没有对每组镜头做适当的白平衡设置。

剪辑软件为电影制作者提供了很多不同类型的转场效果。最好的转场效果就是简单的剪切和溶解。可以多看看你喜欢的电影或者电视节目，你会发现转场效果通常只有剪切和溶解。

一旦你完成片子的剪辑，务必要给文件做备份，如果全部内容都完成了，就可以做一个快速的小尺寸的渲染。

音乐和音响效果设计

（1）音乐

所有视觉效果的部分都处理好后，你就应该考虑音乐内容，以及什么地方需要加入音响效果来给表演增加效果。音乐和音响效果是对片子的最后润色。恰当的音乐可以增强片子的情感、气氛，而音响效果则可以给片子营造的视觉效果增加真实的感觉。

你可以将音乐及音响效果部分交给专业的音响效果设计公司或工作室来做，他们要根据片子的最后版本来做设计。根据你所要求的音乐风格他们会提供给你几段加上音响效果的音乐小样，然后会制作出整个片子的音轨。当他们的工作完成后会给你一个立体声的 wav 文件，你可以把音轨放入 Premiere 里进行编辑。

（2）音响效果

除了音乐，你还需要给影片添加适当的音响效果来丰富音频的内容、提高音频的质量。例如，一个人正跑在泥泞的路面上，脚每次踩到地面的时候你都需要听见扑哧扑哧的声响。

有两种方法可以获取音轨的音响效果：调用音响效果库里现成的音响效果或自己来录制音响效果。在线音响效果库，如 www.sounddogs.com、www.sound-ideas.com、www.soundfx.com，它们在网络上提供大量的音响效果，你可以在线收听或下载。如果你需要给你的影片制作完全原创的独特的音响效果，你就不得不自己来录制了。大部分的声音都可以在现实场景里创造出来。比如，如果你想要一个繁忙的街道的声音，你就可以把麦克风放到主干道上把声音直接录下来就可以了。

在 Premiere 里，我们把音乐放在一个音频层上，把其他的音响效果放在其他的几个层上。然后我们听一遍再继续调整音响效果的音量级别。当音响效果都处理好了之后，就可以准备把整个文件输出到磁带或胶片上。

最终合成

整个片子的内容都完成了，在不同的层上放置动画并调整颜色，背景放在最底层，标题或动画特效放在顶层，音乐和音响效果都已经做好并放置进来。现在做最后的合成，一帧一帧地来检查，然后将所有内容渲染输出成电影格式的文件。如果某一帧出现问题，不要担心，每个片子在制作的时候总会出现一些小问题。重新输出那一帧，再重新输出那个镜头，接着在编辑软件里重新创建一个文件。这里我提供了几个合成的关键方法以供参考。

（1）分层

通常某个特殊的效果是要结合好几个独立层的动作制作出来的。为了实现各种特定的分层视差效果，你应该使用 Adobe After Effects 软件来制作，其他的软件比如 Autodesk 公司的 Combustion 也同样不错。After Effects 可以理解成为 Adobe Photoshop 和 Adobe Premiere 这两种软件的合成品。和 Photoshop 一样，After Effects 可以通过透明通道将每层上不想要观众看到的内容移除。

（2）透明度

在实际操作中分层处理的另一个好处就是你可以在某一层做出透明的视觉效果。这本来也是很容易做出来的，不论关注的对象是动态的还是静态的。但是，如果你没有 After Effects 或类似的软件，你可以在 Photoshop 之类的软件里得到相同的效果，然后用一个像 Adobe Premiere 这类的影片编辑软件来做合成。

（3）循环动画

如果你想表现一个角色从屏幕很远的右边走到很远的左边，可以用一个重复的走路循环动画和一个很长并平移的背景，以及一棵树做前景遮挡就可以了。数字制作技术很擅长这种方式。由于场景是分层制作的，所以循环走要放在上层而背景要放在底层。这样就会给人一种错觉，仿佛摄像机是跟随角色拍摄的。

（4）景深

最后，一个镜头的场景深度可以通过控制景深来实现。这实际上就意味着在不同的层之间改变焦点。在保持前景动作清晰的同时也就是将背景放在焦点之外，反之亦然，前景模糊则背景就清晰。

（5）标题和特效

大部分动画片都有或需要一个开场序列来展示片子的标题。这些标题序列可以是完全静态的或动态的，也可以是动画的，任何形式都可以，你需要试着尽量让标题符合或加强片子的主题。

大部分的标题卡是在 Photoshop 里制作的。标题卡文件要跟片子的视频尺寸大小相同，但是由于 NTSC 制式的视频是长方形像素而 Photoshop 是正方形像素的，因此你需要调整图片的像素形状。动画片的标题序列都是在 After Effects 里制作的。

你的标题设计完成后，你应该把图片导出成 RGB 文件类型，这样合成或剪辑时就能直接使用了。我们通常用 tga 或 tif 格式的文件，它们是未经压缩的图片格式。

所有重要的图像和文字都需要放置在安全区域内或安全框内。每一台电视机都会将投射出来的完整图像或多或少地裁切掉一部分。标题安全框就是所有文字要保持在内的区域，动作安全框就是重要的图形或动作保持在内的边界线。合成和剪辑软件在使用的时候都会提供这些边界线。

标题卡的时间设置也非常重要。你要保证大部分观众有足够的时间来阅读屏幕上的全部文字，同时又不会因为文字出现的时间过长而厌倦。实际操作会帮助你决定在屏幕上出现标题的适当时间长度。

（6）演职员名单

有三种制作演职员名单的基本方式：①可以是单独的图形卡；②用剪辑软件来制作；③用合成软件来创建。如果你的名单里只需要出现几个名字，你就可以用一些图形卡并在剪辑软件或合成软件里给它们设定时间。其他的，你就可以用一个滚动的演职员名单。如果你发现做出来的效果跟你所设想的不一样，那就研究其他的技术和方法来使你达到目的。

Unit 5　International Animation Festival
第 5 单元　国际动画节

5.1　Annecy International Animation Film Festival (France)
昂西国际动画节（法国）

Text

The Annecy International Animation Festival (Festival International du Film d'Animation d'Annecy) was created in 1960 and takes place at the beginning of June in the town of Annecy, France. Initially occurring every two years, the festival became annual in 1998. It is one of the four international animated film festivals sponsored by the International Animated Film Association.

The festival is a competition open to all animated films of various techniques. The five categories of these animated films are feature films for over-one-hour feature length animation made on film; short films for short animation made on film or video; commissioned films for education films, advertising films; films produced for television; graduation films for animations made by students from schools or universities; films made for the internet (since 2002).

Throughout the six-day animation festival, in addition to the competing films projected in various cinemas of the city, an open-air night projection is organized on Pâquier, in the centre of town, amongst the lake and with the mountains. According to the topic of the festival, classic or recent films are projected upon the giant screen. In 2012, Tram won the short film award while Crulic: The Path to Beyond won the feature film award. The capacity to present and promote animation in all its different forms has made Annecy a world-wide point of reference for the animation industry.

Words and phrases

annual　年度的，每年的
sponsor　赞助，发起，主办
International Animated Film Association　国际动画协会
competition　竞赛，比赛
commission　委任，委托
graduation film　毕业电影
project　投射
present　提出，介绍
promote　促进，提升

Web links

www.annecy.org

Translation of text

昂西国际动画节于 1960 年 6 月初，在法国的一个小镇昂西创建。最初每两年举办一次，从 1998 年开始改为每年一次。它是由国际动画电影协会主办的四个国际动画电影节之一。

动画节的竞赛单元向所有的动画电影开放，不限制技术手段。动画节设有几大评奖种类，分别为一小时以上的动画长片、动画短片、商业动画片（包括教育片和广告片）、电视动画片、在校学生毕业作品和网络动画片（从 2002 年开始）。

在为期 6 天的动画节里，除了在全市各家电影院展映竞赛作品外，晚上还在市中心群山环绕的湖边放映露天电影。根据动画节的主题，经典电影或最新影片也会在大型屏幕上播放。2012 年，《电车》获得了最佳动画短片奖，《超越之路》获得了最佳动画长片奖。昂西国际动画节在表现和提高各种不同的艺术表现形式方面的能力和水平，成为世界动画产业的参照标准。

5.2 Hiroshima International Animation Festival (Japan)

广岛国际动画节（日本）

Text

The Hiroshima International Animation Festival is a biannual animation festival hosted in Hiroshima, Japan. The festival was found in 1985 by Association International du Film d' Animation (ASIFA). The city of Hiroshima was one of the sights of nuclear bombings in 1945 at the end of World War II and it was chosen to inspire thoughts of unity through the arts. Under the spirit of LOVE & PEACE, the festival has been dedicating to the advancement of visual media art culture in general, by promoting international cross-cultural exchanges through the development of animation art.

Hiroshima Festival is a comprehensive animation festival, featuring competition programs to choose the Grand Prix, Hiroshima Prize and other prizes out of many latest animation shorts submitted from around the world. The festival also offers many special programs including retrospectives of masters and talented filmmakers, feature animations, high quality student works, as well as seminars, symposiums, workshops, exhibitions, and educational film market, etc. With its outstanding international programs and administration, the festival is highly recognized not only within animation field but also throughout the media art society.

The festival is now considered one of the most respected animated festivals, along with Annecy International Animated Film Festival, Ottawa International Animation Festival, and Zagreb World Festival of Animated Films.

Words and phrases

biannual 一年两次的
host 主办
nuclear bombing 原子弹爆炸
cross-cultural exchang 跨文化交流
comprehensive 综合的，全面的
Grand Prix 大奖，头等奖
retrospective 回顾展
seminar 讨论会，研讨班
symposium 座谈会，专题讨论会
workshop 研讨会，讲习班，工作坊
administration 管理，行政

Web links

www.hiroanim.org

Translation of text

广岛国际动画节是一个在日本广岛举办的一年两次的动画节。该动画节是由国际动画协会于1985年创建的。广岛是1945年第二次世界大战末期遭受原子弹袭击的城市之一，选择这座城市是想通过艺术传递和谐的主题。以爱与和平为理念，这个动画节致力于推动视觉媒体艺术文化的进步，通过发展动画艺术促进国际跨文化交流。

广岛动画节是一个综合性的动画节，设有竞赛单元，从世界各地提交上来的众多最新动画短片中评出竞赛大奖、广岛奖和其他奖项。动画节还提供了很多特别的节目，包括大师和优秀电影导演的作品回顾展，动画长片、高质量的学生作品的展映，以及研讨会、座谈会、展览、教育电影市场等。凭借其出色的国际策划和管理，广岛国际动画节不仅在动画领域，而且在整个媒体艺术界已被高度认可。

广岛国际动画节和昂西国际动画节、渥太华国际动画节、萨格勒布世界动画电影节一样，现在被认为是最受人推崇的动画节之一。

5.3 Zagreb World Festival of Animated Film (Croatia)

萨格勒布国际动画电影节（克罗地亚）

Text

The Zagreb World Festival of Animated Film, also known as Animafest Zagreb is traditionally the second oldest festival in Europe. Approved by ASIFA (International Animated Film Association) and founded by the City of Zagreb and the production studio Zagreb Film the first World Festival of Animated Film was held in June 1972. In the course of its forty-year-old history it has systematically been following world animation production through a number of films in competition and out of competition. Built on the tradition of the Zagreb School of Animation, Animafest, the festival oriented towards auteur film, has made a reputation of being one of the most significant events in the domain of animated film.

Animafest Zagreb takes place every year in spring time, each odd-numbered year is devoted to feature film and even-numbered one to short film. Festival awards include prizes given in the Main Competition, Student Films Competition, Children Films, Educational Films, Commercials, Music Videos and Films Made for the Internet. The Lifetime Achievement Award, which is unique for animation film festivals, was established in 1986. An award for outstanding contribution to the theory of animation was added in 2002.

Words and phrases

    systematically   有系统地，有组织地
    in competition   正式竞赛单元
    out of competition   非竞赛单元
    auteur film   作者电影
    reputation   名声，名誉，声望
    domain   领域，产业

Web links

    www.animafest.hr

Translation of text

萨格勒布国际动画电影节（也被称为 Animafest 萨格勒布）是欧洲第二古老的动画节。动画节由国际动画协会批准创办，并于 1972 年 6 月创立。在其 40 年的历程中，通过大量的正式竞赛单元和非竞赛单元影片，动画节一直系统地跟随世界动画制作的步伐。建立在萨格勒布动画学派的基础上，动画节面向作者电影，在动画电影领域取得了良好的声誉。

萨格勒布国际动画电影节每年春季的时候举办，奇数年致力于长片电影，偶数年则专注于动画短片。动画节的奖项包括主竞赛单元、学生电影竞赛、儿童电影、教育片、商业广告、音乐短片和网络电影。1986 年，动画节设立了终身成就奖，这在动画领域尚属首次。2002 年加入了针对动画理论的杰出贡献奖。

5.4 Ottawa International Animation Festival (Canada)
渥太华国际动画节（加拿大）

Text

The Ottawa International Animation Festival (OIAF) was founded in 1975 by the Canadian Film Institute, and celebrated every other year in Ottawa, Canada since 1976. In 2005, the festival moved from a biennial to an annual festival. The OIAF creates a gathering place for North American animation professionals and enthusiasts around the world to ponder the craft and business of animation. It also provides their international colleagues with a unique opportunity to gain an appreciation for and access to the North American scene.

The OIAF is the largest animation festival in North America, attracting filmmakers, animators, film buffs, art lovers and animation fans. During this festival, many important events, such as screenings, panels and workshops, are open to the public. Unlike other festival of this kind, the OIAF actively encourages participation of the general public and unites the artists, industry personnel, art students and cartoon fans into one vibrant hub. It also seeks to provide a means of inter-linking the regional, national, and international animation communities. The festival exists in part to provide an artistic and commercial forum wherein aesthetic and artistic excellence, as well as commercial expertise, can be shared and exchanged among these various communities.

Words and phrases

Canadian Film Institute 加拿大电影协会
enthusiast 爱好者
ponder 思索，考虑
industry personnel 行业人员
commercial expertise 商业知识

Web links

www.ottawafestivals.ca

Translation of text

渥太华国际动画节（OIAF）由加拿大电影学院于1975年创办，自1976年以来，每隔一年在加拿大渥太华举办。2005年，动画节从两年举办一次改为每年一次。动画节为北美动画专业人士和全世界的动画爱好者创造了一个平台，来探讨动画的制作行业和商业运作。它还给国际同行一个欣赏北美风景的独特机会。

渥太华国际动画节是北美最大的动画节，吸引了众多的制片人、动画师、影迷、艺术爱好者及动漫迷们。在动画节期间有许多重要的事件，如电影放映、研讨会、讲习班，这些都是向公众开放的。与其他同类的动画节不同，渥太华国际动画节积极鼓励市民参与，并将许多艺术家、行业人员、艺术类学生和卡通迷联合成一个充满活力的中心。它为不同地区、国家和国际的动漫交流提供了一种方法。动画节在某种程度上还提供艺术和商业论坛，不同文化背景的审美观点和优秀艺术品以及商业知识在这里可以共享和交流。

5.5 Holland Animation Film Festival
荷兰动画电影节

Text

Holland Animation Film Festival (HAFF) is an international festival for animated film, founded in

1985. The festival takes place over a period of five days at several locations in the city of Utrecht, the Netherlands. The festival started as a biennial festival and became a yearly event in 2009 so it can offer an even more up-to-date programme and really monitor developments as they unfold. The jubilee program covered everything from good music videos, hilarious cartoons, and conventional films to spectacular computer animations.

The festival provides a national and international platform for animation. It is a national and international meeting place and source of inspiration for animation professionals and rising talent and it promotes animated film as an attractive cultural leisure pursuit to all possible target groups. The festival highlights the latest developments and new talent, organizes competitions and presents thematic programmes and retrospectives, talk shows, master classes, debates and an educational programme. There are international competitions for features, shorts and web films.

HAFF is known for its idiosyncratic approach and its choice for quality and innovation. Striking was the increased number, quality and variety of the submitted work for the Holland Animation Film Festival. These highlights thus present the state of the art of commissioned or so-called applied animation.

Words and phrases

up-to-date　最新的，最近的
hilarious　滑稽的，热闹的
inspiration　灵感，启发
idiosyncratic　特殊的
striking　显著的，惊人的
applied animation　实用动画

Web links

www.haff.nl

Translation of text

　　荷兰动画电影节（HAFF）是一个国际动画电影节，成立于1985年。电影节为期五天，举办地点在荷兰乌德勒支市。电影节刚开始是两年举办一次，在2009年改为一个年度节日，这样就可以提供最新的节目及密切关注最新的事态发展。庆典节目包罗万象，包括优秀的动画音乐录像、热闹的卡通片、传统动画片，以及令人赞不绝口的电脑动画。

　　荷兰动画电影节为荷兰和国际的动画交流提供了良好的平台。这是荷兰或国际动画专业人士、人才的集会和灵感的来源，并将动画电影作为一个有吸引力的文化休闲追求推向可能的目标群体。电影节强调的最新发展和新的人才，组织竞赛，并举办专题节目和展览、座谈会、大师班、辩论和教学项目。电影节设有针对动画长片、动画短片和网络动画的竞赛单元。

　　动画节因其特殊的方法及对作品质量的选择和创新而闻名。荷兰动画电影节上展出的作品，无论在数量、质量还是种类上都是惊人的。这些作品突出表现了商业动画或所谓的实用动画的现状。

Unit 6　Famous Animation Studios
第 6 单元　著名动画工作室

6.1　Pixar Animation Studios
皮克斯动画工作室

Text

Pixar Animation Studios is an award-winning animation studio famous for its computer-animated film shorts and for the feature films that it produces in conjunction with Disney, who splits costs of production and distribution by covering all distribution issues while Pixar handles production. Pixar has so far produced thirteen films.

Initially, when Pixar was a high-end computer hardware company whose core product was the Pixar Image Computer, a system primarily sold to government agencies and the medical community. One of the buyers of Pixar Image Computers was Disney Studios, which was using the device as part of their projects, using the machine and custom software to migrate the laborious ink and paint part of the 2D animation process. When this led to a multimillion dollar deal with Disney, Pixar's future in animation was established with the production of Toy Story.

Since its incorporation, Pixar has been responsible for many important breakthroughs in the application of computer graphics (CG) for filmmaking. Consequently, the company has attracted some of the world's finest talent in this area. Pixar's technical and creative teams have collaborated since 1986 to develop a wealth of production software used in-house to create its movies and further the state of the art in CG movie making. This proprietary technology allows the production of animated images of a quality, richness and vibrancy that are unique in the industry, and above all, allows the director to precisely control the end results in a way that is exactly right for the story. Pixar continues to invest heavily in its software systems and believes that further advancements will lead to additional productivity and quality improvements in the making of its computer animated films.

Major works:
Toy Story (1995)
A Bug's Life (1998)
Toy Story 2 (1999)
Monsters Inc. (2001)
Finding Nemo (2003)
The Incredibles (2004)

Cars (2006)
Ratatouille (2007)
WALL·E (2008)
Up (2009)
Toy Story 3 (2010)
Cars 2 (2011)
Brave (2012)

Words and phrases

award-winning   备受赞誉的，成功的
distribution   发行，经销，分配
high-end   高端的，高档的
migrate   迁移
laborious   勤劳的，艰苦的，费劲的
incorporation   注册成立，合并
breakthrough   突破，突破性进展
collaborate   合作，协作
in-house   内部的

Web links

www.pixar.com

Translation of text

皮克斯动画工作室是一个屡获殊荣的动画制作公司，因其与迪士尼合作完成的诸多电脑动画短片和动画长片而闻名，在两者的合作中，迪士尼负责制作经费及宣传发行部分，皮克斯负责影片的制作部分。皮克斯至今已制作了 13 部动画电影。

最初，皮克斯是一个高端的计算机硬件公司，其核心产品是皮克斯图像电脑，是主要出售给政府机构和医学界的一种系统。皮克斯图像电脑的买家之一是迪士尼，迪士尼用这些硬件设备作为项目的一部分，用这些设备和定制软件来完成二维动画制作过程中的上色和绘制部分，替代原有的手绘方式。这样就与迪士尼达成了数百万美元的交易，之后皮克斯在动画上的发展从《玩具总动员》开始。

皮克斯加入迪士尼以来，一直专注于研发计算机图形（CG）在电影制作领域中的应用。因此，公司吸引了一批在这方面有天赋的人才。皮克斯的技术与创意团队的合作始于 1986 年，开发了一系列先进的 CG 电影制作的内部软件。这项专利技术可以生成高质量逼真的三维图形，这在同行中是独一无二的，并且让导演能够以精确的方式来完成故事的表现。皮克斯将继续在其软件系统研发上加大投入，而且会使其电脑动画电影制作的额外生产力和质量有所改进。

主要作品：

玩具总动员（1995）

虫虫危机（1998）

玩具总动员2（1999）
怪物公司（2001）
海底总动员（2003）
超人总动员（2004）
汽车总动员（2006）
料理鼠王（2007）
机器人瓦力（2008）
飞屋环游记（2009）
玩具总动员3（2010）
汽车总动员2（2011）
勇敢传说（2012）

6.2 Blue Sky Studios

蓝天工作室

Text

Blue Sky Studios is an American CGI-animation studio which specializes in high-resolution, computer-generated character animation and rendering. It is owned by 20th Century Fox and located in Greenwich, Connecticut. In addition to their feature-length animated films, including the Ice Age series, Robots (2005), Horton Hears a Who! (2008), and Rio (2011), Blue Sky has worked on many high-profile films, primarily in the integration of live-action with computer-generated animation.

Blue Sky was founded in February 1987. Throughout the late 1980s and 1990s, the studio concentrated on the production of television commercials and visual effects for film. Using their proprietary animation pipeline, the studio produced over 200 spots for clients. In August 1997, 20th Century Fox's Los Angeles based effects company, VIFX, acquired Blue Sky Studios to form VIFX. The new company produced visual effects for films such as The X-Files, Blade, Armageddon, Titanic and Alien Resurrection. In 1998, Blue Sky Studios realized long unfulfilled dreams and produced the Academy Awarded animated short film, Bunny.

In 1999, Fox decided to leave visual effects business, and considered selling Blue Sky next. At the time, the studio got the opportunity with the Ice Age script to turn it into a comedy. In 2002, Ice Age was released to a great critical and commercial success. The film got a nomination for an Academy Award for Best Animated Feature, and established Blue Sky as the third studio, after Pixar and DreamWorks, to launch a successful CGI franchise.

Major works:

Ice Age (2002)

Robots (2005)

Ice Age: The Meltdown (2006)

Horton Hears a Who! (2008)
Ice Age: Dawn of the Dinosaurs (2009)
Rio (2011)
Ice Age: Continental Drift (2012)
Epic (2013)

Words and phrases

high-profile　高知名度的，引人注目的
television commercial　电视广告
proprietary　专有的，专利的
pipeline　流水线，工艺流程，管线
spots　插播广告
nomination　提名
franchise　特许经营，专营权

Web links

www.blueskystudios.com

Translation of text

　　蓝天工作室是一个美国的电脑动画工作室，专门从事高分辨率电脑生成的角色动画和渲染。它隶属于 20 世纪福克斯电影公司，工作室位于康涅狄格州的格林威治。除了《冰河世纪》系列、《机器人历险记》(2005)、《霍顿与无名氏》(2008)、《里约大冒险》(2011) 这些动画长片外，蓝天工作室还参与了许多高知名度的电影，主要是制作电脑动画与真人动作的合成。

　　蓝天工作室始建于 1987 年 2 月。在整个 20 世纪 80 年代末和 90 年代，该工作室主要制作电视广告和电影的视觉特效。使用其专有的动画制作流程，该工作室为客户制作了超过 200 部的插播广告。在 1997 年 8 月，20 世纪福克斯公司位于洛杉矶的特效公司 VIFX 收购了蓝天工作室组建了 VIFX。新公司为很多电影制作特效，如《X 档案》、《刀锋战士》、《绝世天劫》、《泰坦尼克号》和《异形 4》。1998 年，蓝天工作室终于实现了夙愿，动画短片《兔子》终于获得了奥斯卡最佳动画短片奖。

　　1999 年，福克斯决定停止视觉特效业务，并考虑出售蓝天工作室。在这个时候，工作室得到了将《冰河世纪》的剧本制作成喜剧片的机会。2002 年，《冰河世纪》上映并取得了商业上的成功。这部影片得到了奥斯卡最佳动画奖的提名，并使得蓝天工作室成为继皮克斯和梦工厂之后的第三个成功拥有 CGI 特许经营权的工作室。

　　主要作品：
《冰河世纪》(2002)
《机器人历险记》(2005)
《冰河世纪 2：消融》(2006)
《霍顿与无名氏》(2008)
《冰河世纪 3：恐龙的黎明》(2009)

《里约大冒险》（2011）

《冰河世纪 4：大陆漂移》（2012）

《森林战士》（2013）

6.3 Studio Ghibli
吉卜力工作室

Text

Studio Ghibli is a Japanese animation studio, led by one of animation's greatest creators, Hayao MIYAZAKI. Studio Ghibli began in June 1985 after the success of Nausicaa of the Valley of the Wind with funding by Tokuma Shoten. The company's logo features the character Totoro from Miyazaki's film My Neighbor Totoro. The studio creates very high quality animated movies, which is rather unique, since most Japanese animation studios depend on TV series or OVAs. They consistently beat Disney movies in box office revenues in Japan and have received numerous awards. Miyazaki and Ghibli movies are well respected and loved by all Japanese people, children and adults alike.

Ghibli was established in 1985, to make the film, "Laputa: The Castle in the Sky". However, the beginning of the studio can be dated back to 1983, when Tokuma Shoten (Tokuma Publishing, Co., Ltd) decided to produce "Nausicaa of the Valley of Wind". Tokuma is a Japanese publishing company which publishes "Animage", an animation magazine, in which Miyazaki had been serializing the manga "Nausicaa" since 1982. After the success of "Nausicaa", Tokuma and Miyazaki decided to make their second movie, "Laputa", and they established Studio Ghibli. Ghibli means "hot wind blowing through the Sahara Desert". The name was used for Italian scouting airplanes during World War II. Miyazaki, who loves airplanes (and Italy), named his studio after it.

Miyazaki is an animator, first and foremost. He personally checks almost all the key animation, and often redraws roughs when he thinks they aren't good enough or characters aren't "acting right." This isn't the typical way in which a director works. Miyazaki feels this hands-on approach is the only way for him to make the films he wants to make.

Miyazaki had been rather skeptical about the use of computers in anime. The first time Ghibli used CG was in "Pom Poko", in the scene where the camera panned the library shelves. Such a scene is very difficult and time consuming for animators to do, and yet, does not require creativity and therefore is boring for animators to do. "Whisper of the Heart" used digital composition in the fantasy scenes, meaning that elements (animated by traditional means) of a scene were composed using a computer, "On Your Mark" used some computer generated images, and "Mononoke Hime" used computers extensively. Ghibli bought several Silicon Graphics workstations and set up a CG Division.

Studio Ghibli has produced seventeen feature films, beginning with Castle in the Sky in 1986. It was followed by Grave of the Fireflies (1988), My Neighbor Totoro (1988), Kiki's Delivery Service (1989), Only Yesterday (1991), Porco Rosso (1992), Pom Poko (1994), Whisper of the Heart (1995),

Princess Mononoke (1997), My Neighbors the Yamadas (1999), Spirited Away (2001), The Cat Returns (2002), Howl's Moving Castle (2004), Tales from Earthsea (2006), Ponyo (2008), Arrietty (2010), and From Up on Poppy Hill (2011). Sixteen of the films received both critical and financial success, with the notable exception being Tales from Earthsea, which, in spite of its commercial success, achieved less critical praise than Ghibli's other productions. Many anime features created by Studio Ghibli have won the Animage Anime Grand Prix award and three have won the Japan Academy Prize for Animation of the Year. In 2002, Spirited Away won a Golden Bear and an Oscar for Best Animated Feature.

Words and phrases

unique 独特的，独一无二的
skeptical 好怀疑的，多疑的
Silicon Graphics workstation 硅谷图形工作站

Web links

www.studioghibli.net

Translation of text

吉卜力工作室是一个由动画大师宫崎骏所带领的日本动画工作室。吉卜力工作室于1985年6月由德间书店投资的《风之谷》获得成功后开始组建。公司的标志形象是宫崎骏的动画电影《龙猫》里的龙猫。大多数日本动画工作室的业务主要依靠动画电视剧或原创剧场版动画，而吉卜力工作室则主要制作高品质的动画电影，这是非常独特的。在日本他们的作品在票房上始终能够击败迪士尼的动画片，并且获得了无数的奖项。宫崎骏和吉卜力工作室的动画片受到所有日本人民，包括儿童和成人的尊敬和爱戴。

吉卜力是于1985年为制作《天空之城》而成立的。但是更早的工作可追溯到1983年，也就是德间书店（德间出版有限公司）决定投资制作《风之谷》的时候。德间书店是日本的一个出版公司，它出版了动画杂志《Animage》，在这本杂志里宫崎骏从1982年开始发表连载漫画《风之谷》。在《风之谷》成功之后，德间书店和宫崎骏决定制作他们的第二部电影《天空之城》，这样他们就建立了吉卜力工作室。吉卜力的意思是"通过撒哈拉大沙漠吹来的热风"。这个名字被用于第二次世界大战期间意大利的侦察飞机。宫崎骏很喜欢飞机以及意大利，所以用这个名字来命名工作室。

宫崎骏认为自己首先以及最重要的身份是一个动画师。他亲自检查几乎所有的关键动画，当他认为画得不够好或角色没有"表演正确"的时候，经常会亲自重新绘制草稿。这些通常不是导演的工作。宫崎骏认为用这种手绘的方式是能做出他想做的电影的唯一方法。

宫崎骏曾经对使用电脑来做动画持非常怀疑的态度。吉卜力第一次使用电脑技术是在《百变狸猫》中，用于摄像机在图书馆书架之间平移的场景里。这样的镜头对动画师来说是非常困难又耗时的工作，不仅如此还极其没有创造力，因此对动画师来说非常的枯燥。《侧耳倾听》在幻想镜头里用到了数字合成技术，这就是说一个镜头所有的元素（用传统二维动画手法制作的）用电脑进行合成，《On Your Mark》里用到了一些电脑生成的图像，而到了《幽灵公主》的时候则较多地使用电脑来制作。吉卜力购买了好几个硅谷图形工作站，并成立了电脑动画部门。

从1986年的《天空之城》开始，吉卜力工作室已经制作了17部动画长片。它们依次是《萤火虫之墓》

(1988)、《龙猫》(1988)、《魔女宅急便》(1989)、《岁月的童话》(1991)、《红猪》(1992)、《百变狸猫》(1994)、《侧耳倾听》(1995)、《幽灵公主》(1997)、《我的邻居山田君》(1999)、《千与千寻》(2001)、《猫的报恩》(2002)、《哈尔的移动城堡》(2004)、《地海战记》(2006)、《悬崖上的金鱼公主》(2008)、《借东西的小人阿莉埃蒂》(2010) 和《来自虞美人之坡》(2011)。除了《地海战记》，其他 16 部电影都获得了艺术上和票房上的成功。虽然《地海战记》在商业上很成功，但在艺术水准上不如吉卜力的其他作品。由吉卜力工作室制作的许多动画获得了 Animage 动漫大奖最高奖项，并有三部动画获得了日本学院奖年度最佳动画奖。在 2002 年，《千与千寻》获得了金熊奖和奥斯卡最佳动画长片奖。

6.4 Aardman Animation Studios
阿德曼动画工作室

Text

Aardman Animations, Ltd., also known as Aardman Studios is a British animation studio based in Bristol, United Kingdom. It was founded in 1972 by animators David Sproxton and Peter Lord, and had molded a reputation as one of the world's top animation studios. It has achieved widespread recognition for its stop-motion animation techniques, filming three-dimensional objects frame-by-frame, and especially its series of Wallace and Gromit short films, including the Oscar award-winning The Wrong Trousers and A Close Shave. Led by cofounders Peter Lord and David Sproxton, Aardman has branched out into feature films, including the 2001 success, Chicken Run, through a $150 million, four-film production agreement with DreamWorks. That agreement also includes the first full-length Wallace and Gromit film, released in 2005, and "Flushed Away," the studio's first CG (computer generated) animated film. Yet a primary source of the private company's revenues has long been its groundbreaking production for the advertising industry.

Words and phrases

reputation　名誉，声望
recognition　认可，赞誉
cofounder　共同创办人，创始人
branched out into　分成，分支成
groundbreaking　开创性的

Web links

www.aardman.com

Translation of text

阿德曼动画公司，也被称为阿德曼工作室，是一个总部设在英国布里斯托尔的动画工作室。工作室于 1972 年由动画师大卫·史保斯顿和彼得·洛伊德共同建立，并赢得了世界顶级动画工作室之一的声誉。

工作室因其定格动画技术，即逐帧拍摄三维实体模型的动画方式，得到了广泛的认可，尤其是《超级无敌掌门狗》系列短片，其中《裤子错了》和《九死一生》获得了奥斯卡最佳动画短片奖。在联合创始人彼得·洛伊德和大卫·史保斯顿的带领下，阿德曼还涉足动画长片，包括2001年成功的《小鸡快跑》，获得超过1.5亿美元的票房，并与梦工厂签订了制作四部动画作品的协议。协议里也包括2005年第一部完整长度的《超级无敌掌门狗》电影，以及工作室的第一部电脑动画电影《冲走小老鼠》。但是工作室的主要收入长期以来还是依靠广告行业的原创作品。

Appendix: Glossary
附录：动画专业术语表

A

academy awards 奥斯卡金像奖，美国电影艺术与科学学院于 1928 年设立的奖项，每年颁给表现杰出的电影工作者

action 动作，动画角色所做的移、转、跳、跑等各种姿态

adaptation 改编，将故事、小说、戏剧或其他适合通过电影、动画媒体来处理的作品搬上银幕

animate 动画，使有生气

animated feature 动画长片，90 分钟以上长度的动画

animatic 动态故事板、动画预演，将故事板按时间分配及顺序进行动态影像化并制作出样片的过程

animation camera 动画摄影机，一种装有停顿马达的摄影机，可单格拍摄，拍摄时装在动画摄影台上，可垂直移动，以改变影像的大小或产生变焦的效果

animation film 动画电影

animator 原画师、动画设计者，或为动画制作者的通称

animatronic 动画机械模型偶，动画道具中装有机械骨架的角色，一般使用遥控器来控制

anime 日本风格的动画

anticipation 预备动作、动画预期

anticlimax 反高潮，在电影最后解决冲突时，没有出现观众所期待的情节，使现众感到失望的情节设计效果

armature 骨架、支架，制作偶动画角色用的内部结构

art director 美术指导、艺术总监

assistant animator 助理动画师，在主动画师（lead animator）的带领下进行关键帧的绘制

asynchronism 音画分离，指影片上的声音和影像不相符

atmosphere sketch 气氛草图，确定影片场景气氛的草

B

B. P.（bot pegs） 下定位，定位孔或者定位点位于动画纸下方的定位方法

background（BG） 背景

background artist 背景艺术家

batch process 批处理

bitmap 位图

blue screen　蓝屏

bones　骨骼，三维动画中用骨骼来对角色模型进行控制

BRK DN（B. D.）（breakdown）　过渡位置，是一种特殊的关键帧，它与临近关键帧在时间上保持一定的比例关系

C

C. U.（close-up）　特写，影视动画或者摄影艺术中的一种镜头景别

camera angle　摄影机角度

camera movement　摄影机运动，指电影摄影机的运动，目的在于跟随一个动作，或改变被摄场景、人物或物体的呈现方式

camera shake　晃镜头，是指拍摄过程中摄像机机身做上下、左右、前后摇摆的拍摄

camera tracking　摄影机跟踪，可能轻松地捕捉实拍时摄影机的运动轨迹，这样虚拟摄影机就可以将三维造型逼真地放置在实景中

CEL/celluloid　赛璐珞、透明片、电影胶片材料

character-based animation　角色动画

character arc　角色性格曲线，体现为在故事变化过程中，角色人物最终克服各种局限，使得情境发生改变

character designer　角色设计师

claymation　黏土动画，定格动画的一种，它由逐帧拍摄制作而成，它是用黏土或橡皮泥等可塑材质来制作人物，一般运用金属骨架来控制角色的造型和姿态

clean-up　清稿，是手绘动画制作流程中的一个部分，主要对通过铅笔稿审查的动画进行清理和重新临摹，使画面更为统一

click track　节拍音轨，在录音时专门用来播放滴答声，作为和录音者之间同步的依据

climax　高潮，指戏剧或电影故事发展中，情绪张力最强的时候，通常一部电影或戏剧故事均有一个或一个以上的高湖

CMYK　印刷四色，分别是青色、洋红色、黄色和黑色

color flash（paint flash）　跳色

color keys（color mark-ups）　色指定

composer　作曲人，负责为影片编写和安排音乐内容的专业人员

compositing　合成，把动画中不同的层和动画元素或特效组合起来，构成一个协调的完整的画面

computer generated imagery（CGI）　计算机生成影像，是计算机数字图像（computer graphics，简称CG）在影视特技领域的应用

concept drawings　概念图，将电影场景中的动作绘制成视觉化的草图方案，可以为团队提供准确的思路

conflict　冲突，是一切剧作的基础，为人物规定出需求，即在剧本中确立他想要达到什么目的后，就可以为这一目标的实现设置障碍，这样就产生了冲突

cross in/cross out　入镜、出镜，指演员自画面的一边进场或朝画面的一边出场

D

dialog（dialogue） 对白及口形
digital ink and paint 数字式描线及上色
director 导演，影视制作团队的领导者，负责把握整部影片的演绎手法、视听风格和动作节奏
dissolve（X. D） 溶解，叠化
distortion 变形
dope sheet 摄影表
double frame 双（画）格
double image 双重影像
doubles 一帧拍两次，在拍摄动画片时，把一张画面拍摄两次用于两幅画帧，常用于传统动画和三维动画制作中
draft 草稿，草图
drawing disc 动画圆盘
dubbing 配音
DV camera 数码摄像机
dwf（drawing） 画，动画纸

E

E. C. U（extreme close up） 大特写
ease-in 渐快、淡入，角色由静止到运动做加速运动
ease-out 渐慢、淡出，角色由运动到静止做减速运动
editing 剪辑
editor 剪辑师
EFT（effect） 特效
enter（in） 入画，指动画人物或者角色进入摄像机可视范围，在镜头中出现
episode 片集，一段故事情节或插曲
exit（moves out, O. S.） 出镜，退场，指动画人物或者角色退出摄像机可视范围，从镜头中消失
experimental animation 实验动画，指非商业的探索性质的动画作品
exposure sheet（X-SHEET） 摄影表，即律表
EXT（exterior） 外面、室外景

F

fade（in/on） 画面淡入，镜头内容由黑场或者完全透明过渡到正常样式
fade（out/off） 画面淡出，镜头内容由正常过渡到黑场或者完全消失
field（FLD） 安全框，防止字幕或者人物做动作时偏出镜头中心范围的指示框
field guide 规格框
Flash 由 Macromedia 公司开发的矢量格式的动画软件

flipbook   翻页动画书、动画手翻书
focal length   焦距
foreground   前景
frame   格、帧、画面
frame by frame   逐帧动画，采用传统动画的制作方式，把要表现的动态分解成一个个的动作，然后逐帧绘制，最后连续播放时形成动画效果
freeze frame   停格、画面冻结

G

gag   笑料、搞笑，动画中主要依靠人物的形象、夸张的表情、肢体动作等来制造笑料
game play   电脑游戏
graphics tablet   数字绘图板

H

hook up   接景、衔接，将两张或者多张过大的背景或者其他画面分开绘制，然后再将其衔接

I

I&P（ink & paint）   描线和着色
inbetween   中间画
inbetweener   中间画师

K

key animator   关键帧画师，在一些成本较高的动画作品中，主要角色的动画将会由动画师组成的专门小组来完成。小组由一个动画监制（supervising animator）、主动画师（lead animator）和助理动画师（assistant animators）组成
keyframe   关键帧，关键帧相当于传统手绘动画中的原画，指角色或者物体运动变化中的关键画面
keys   原画，动画片中交代运动中人物或物体的主要动态之画片，如起步、停止，或变换方向，通常关键动态由动画设计负责绘制

L

layer   图层
layout   构图，指动画影片中背景的设计
layout artist   构图设计师
lead animator   首席动画师
lightbox   灯箱
limited animation   低成本动画，在卡通动画制作过程中，整个影片出现的共同影像，可以在画面中重复使用
line test（pencil test）   铅笔稿测试

lip sync（synchronization） 对口型、唇形对位，指对白与演员的嘴唇动作达到精确的同步效果

live-action film 真人电影（和动画电影相对应的）

M

M. C. U.（mediium close up） 近景

M. S.（medium shot） 中景

MAG TRACK（magnetic sound track） 音轨

model sheet 角色设计、模型表

montage 蒙太奇，一种处理空间与时间的艺术手段，是电影制作过程中决定影像时空的核心技巧

morphing 形变动画，就是由一种形状变形为另一种形状的动画

motion capture 运动捕捉

mouth charts 口形图

N

N. G.（no good） 不好的，作废

O

O. S.（off stage, off scene） 出景

off model 走型

OL/UL（underlay） 前层与中层间的景

OL（overlay） 前层景、覆盖图

out of scene 到画面外

overlap action 重叠动作

P

P. T.（painting） 着色、上色

paint flashes（color flashes） 跳色

palette 调色板，绘图软件中可以选择颜色的调板

pan 移动、平移、摇镜头

papercut 剪纸片，由中国剪纸艺术衍生的一种动画种类

peg bar 定位尺

pencil test 铅笔测试

performance capture 表演捕捉技术，以三维特效的形式将多名演员的面部表情及肢体行为真实地再现

persistence of vision 视觉暂留现象，物体快速运动的影像在人眼中仍能继续保留一小段时间，是动画、电影等视觉媒体形成和传播的最基本的原理

perspective 透视

pixel 像素

pixilation　实体动画，以人或实物为拍摄材料的一种定格动画
plug-in　插件
post-synchronized sound　后期同步录音
pre-production　前期制作
producer　制片人，制作团队的关键成员，负责确保影片在限定的时间和预算范围内进行制作，并从导演的角度支持项目制作，与投资方和发行商谈判所有的发行及相关事宜
production designer　美工师，又称"美术设计"，主要工作任务是统筹设计安排全剧的布景、服装、化妆、道具，设计全剧的、每场戏的色彩基调
protagonist　推动故事往前发展的主要角色
puppet　人偶、木偶、角色模型

R

raytracing　光线跟踪
re-peg　重新定位
render　渲染
RGB　一种色彩标准，是通过对红（R）、绿（G）、蓝（B）三个颜色通道的变化以及它们相互之间的叠加来得到各种颜色
rotoscope　动作转描

S

S.S（screen shake）　画面振动
SC（scene）　镜号、场、场景，由单一镜头或数个镜头组成的戏剧单位
scene planning　场面调度，指对剧场的舞台上一切视觉元素的安排
science-fiction film　科幻片，电影类型的一种，其特色的情节包含了科学奇想
script　文字脚本、剧本，通常记载台词、对话和动作等信息，是使故事脚本或小说详细化的工作，可具体到人物的对话、场景的切换、时间的分割等
secondary action　二级动作，依附在主要动作之下的细微动作
self-line（self-trace line）　色线
sfx（sound effect）　声效、音效
shadow　阴影
shadow puppetry　皮影戏
sheet timer　时间设定，在进行分镜设计的同时，时间设定导演（timing director）将会通过分析动态故事板（animatic）来控制时间,角色的姿势和嘴型将被具体分配到各个帧,然后制作摄影表（exposure sheet）
shot　镜头，摄像机不间断拍摄的一组帧序列，它常被看成一部视频的最小结构单位
silhouette（silo）　剪影，以黑白二色形成图像的"影子"，常用来判断动画片画面、动作表述是否清楚
size comparison　大小比例

slow in　慢进，静止的物体开始移动时由慢而快

slow out　慢出，将要停止的物体则会由快变慢

special effect　特效，不是以直接的电影拍摄技巧获取的镜头，实现的途径是利用计算机软件来生成

speed line　流线、速度线，在动画中表现运动物体，往往在其后面加上几条线来代表快速运动，就是利用这种感觉来强化运动效果，这些线称之为速度线

spin　旋转

staging　演出布局，仔细设计安排动画中的构图、运镜、动作、走位

stop-motion　定格动画，也称停格动画或逐格动画，是一种以手工制作的人物模型为对象，应用摄影技术来制作的一种动画形式

storm out　速转出

storyboard（SAB）　故事板、分镜头台本、分镜头脚本，以草图、绘画或照片，依连戏顺序将影片段落或整部影片的主要动作和叙述流程摘述出来

streaming video　流媒体

stylist　样式设计师，造型师

T

T. A.（top aux）　上辅助定位

T. P.（top pegs）　上定位，定位孔或者定位点位于动画纸上方的定位方法

Texture map　纹理贴图

theme　故事的主题，动画中所表达出的价值观

timeline　时间轴

three-actsructure　三幕结构，指的是剧本的结构，包括开端、中段和结尾三部分

timing　时间选择与控制

tittle　片名，字幕

TR（trace）　描线

trace back　重播

transition　转场，自一场景转至另一场景，或自一段落转至另一段落时，所采用的种种方法

treatment　影视剧的情节大纲，在前期策划阶段用于陈述导演关于影片纲要的文件

truck in　镜头推入

truck out　镜头拉出

tweened frames　补间帧，在补间动画中，由计算机自动运算并补齐的中间帧

tweening　补间动画，在基于关键帧的动画制作法中，由计算机自动运算并补齐的中间帧动画

U

UL（underlay）　中景、后景

V

V.O.（voice over）　旁白、画外音

vector　矢量，计算机显示的图形一般分为两类——矢量图和位图。矢量图与分辨率无关，可无限放大且不失真

vertex　顶点，三维物体中的控制点

vert up　垂直上移

visual effect（VFX）　视觉特效，是影视制作领域中一种通过创造图像和处理真人拍摄范围以外镜头的各种处理方式。通常涉及真人镜头和计算机生成图像（CGI）的合成以创造虚拟的真实场景

voice director　声音导演

W

wipe　转（换）景方式

wireframe　线框建模，线框建模生成的实体模型是由一系列的直线、圆弧、点及自由曲线组成的，描述的是物体的轮廓外形

work print　工作样片

X

X-DISS（X. D.）　两景交融

X-sheet　摄影表

xerox down　缩小

xerox up（xerox paste-ups）　放大

Z

zoom chart　镜头推拉轨迹

zoom in　推进

zoom lens　变焦距镜头

zoom out　拉出

参考文献

[1] Ollie Johnston, Frank Thomas. The Illusion of Life: Disney Animation[M]. Disney Editions, 1995.

[2] Tony White. How to Make Animated Films: Tony White's Complete Masterclass on the Traditional Principals of Animation[M]. Focal Press, 2009.

[3] Mark A. Simon. Producing Independent 2D Character Animation: Making & Selling A Short Film[M].Focal Press, 2003.

[4] Kenny Roy. How to Cheat in Maya 2014: Tools and Techniques for Character Animation[M]. Focal Press, 2013.

[5] Susannah Shaw. Stop Motion: Craft Skills for Model Animation, Second Edition[M]. Focal Press, 2013.

[6] Ken A. Priebe. The Advanced Art of Stop-Motion Animation[M]. Cengage Learning PTR, 2010.

[7] Karen Sullivan. Ideas for the Animated Short: Finding and Building Stories[M]. Focal Press, 2013.

[8] Paul wells. Basics Animation 01: Scriptwriting[M]. AVA Publishing, 2007.

[9] Mark A. Simon. Storyboards: Motion in Art, Third Edition[M].Focal Press, 2006.

[10] John Hart. The Art of the Storyboard: A Filmmaker's Introduction, Second Edition[M]. Focal Press, 2007.

[11] Richard Williams. The Animator's Survival Kit-Revised Edition: A Manual of Methods, Principles and Formulas for Classical, Computer, Games, Stop Motion and Internet Animators[M]. Faber & Faber, 2012.

[12] John Halas. Timing for Animation, Second Edition[M]. Focal Press, 2009.

[13] Mike S. Fowler. Animation Background Layout: From Student to Professional[M]. Fowler Cartooning Arts' 2002.

[14] Robin Beauchamp. Designing Sound for Animation[M]. Focal Press, 2005.

后 记
POSTSCRIPT

  随着现代教育的不断深入发展，专业英语教学始终是高校各学科、专业关注并研究的重点。近年来，国内很多动画院系也相继开设了动画专业英语课程作为专业选修课。这正是当代社会对人才素质要求越来越全面的体现，也是动画教育面对国际交流的必然趋势。这种变化既要求动画专业的学生拥有扎实的专业功底，同时又能运用外语这一工具获取更多的专业信息，具备能够和国际同行进行专业交流的能力。

  作为动画专业教师，为了找到一种适应艺术类学生特点和要求的专业英语教学方法，作者在起笔之前就相关问题请教了英语系的教师，以及动画专业的几位教学经验丰富的同事，深入课堂实践，总结其他院校的优秀经验，在原文选择上遵循着英语知识和动画专业技能两方面都过硬的原则，反复研究、修改，出版了这本教材。

  起笔编写这本教材的时候，我的儿子刚刚满月。家人为了让我安心工作就负责轮流照顾孩子，我陪伴孩子的时间真是少之又少。感谢我的家人这半年多的付出和奉献！感谢我的儿子带给我的快乐和完成书稿的动力！

徐欣